You Can KNIT it All!

65 EASY Hats, Shawls, Pullovers, Blankets, & More

 Get Creative 6

New York

Get Creative 6
An imprint of Mixed Media Resources
19 West 21st St, Suite 601
New York, NY 10010

Editors JACOB SEIFERT,
CARLA SCOTT

Creative Director IRENE LEDWITH

Cover Sample Knitters THERESE CHYNOWETH,
MELISSA DEHNCKE MCGILL, SOPHIA MINAKAIS
SANDI PROSSER

Photography JACK DEUTSCH

Cover Hair and Makeup CYNTHIA ADAMS
———————

Publisher CAROLINE KILMER

President ART JOINNIDES

Chairman JAY STEIN

Copyright © 2024 by Mixed Media Resources

All rights reserved. No part of this publication may be reproduced or used in any form or by any means—graphic, electronic, or mechanical, including photocopying, recording, or information storage-and-retrieval systems—without written permission of the publisher.

The written instructions, photographs, designs, projects, and patterns are intended for the personal, noncommercial use of the retail purchaser and are under federal copyright laws; they are not to be reproduced in any form for commercial use. Permission is granted to photocopy patterns for the personal use of the retail purchaser.

Items created from patterns in this book are for personal use only and are not intended for commercial resale.

A catalog record for this book is available from the Library of Congress.

Manufactured in China

1 3 5 7 9 10 8 6 4 2

First Edition

Contents

Introduction....................8
How to Use This Book..........9
Abbreviations 10

HATS

Super Bulky Hat 12
Rib Duo Watch Cap 14
Staggered Rib Hat 16
Twisted Rib Hat...............18
Basketweave Hat..............20
Toasty Tot Hat................22
Lace Tam......................24
Brioche Watch Cap 26
Torsades Beret 28
Oval Twist Hat & Scarf 30
Accordion Rib Hat & Mitts.....32

SMALL ACCESSORIES

Classic Mittens 36
Heart-Motif Mittens 38
Shell Rib Wristers 40
Fingerless Mitts 42
Sweet Stripes Baby Booties....44
Cabled Baby Booties..........46
Hedgehog Slippers 48
Color-Tipped Slippers.........50
Diamonds Headband 52
Planted Headband............54

SCARVES, SHAWLS & WRAPS

Diagonal Ridge Shawl 56
All Angles Wrap 58
Theatre Shawl 60
Malibu Ripple Shawl 62
Dipper Shawl 64
Peek-a-Boo Lace Shawl 66
Double Swiss Shawl. 69
Shifting Tides Scarf 72
Hound's Tooth Scarf 74
Pocket Scarf. 76
Bow Scarf 78
Textured Cowl 80

SWEATERS & CARDIGANS

Opposites Dolman Pullover 82
Pebble Yoke Pullover. 85
Blaze Pullover 88
Chevron Pullover 91
Snowfall Sweater 94
Honey Pullover 97
Toasty Tot Sweater 100
Pumpkin Spice Pullover 103
Shawl-Collar Cardigan 106
Winter Haze Cardigan. 110
Buttoned Poncho Cardigan 114
Perforated Cardigan 118
Summer Cardigan 122
Garter-Stitch Baby Cardigan . . . 126

BLANKETS

Garter Stripes Blanket 129
Stained Glass Blanket. 132

Bunny Buddy Blanket 134
Stronger Together Blanket 136
Gridded Blanket 138
Chevron Pop Blanket 140
Purl Stitch Snowflake Blanket .. 142
Turtle Lace Blanket 144
Garden Patch Lapghan 146
Garter Gingham Blanket 148
Candy Cabin Afghan & Pillow ... 150
Shifting Chevron Blanket 154

HOME & OTHER
Garter Stitch Basket 156
Textured Washcloths 158
Potted Plant Cozies 160
On the Market 162
Cup Cozy Quartet 164
Dog Coat 166

TECHNIQUES & HOW-TO
Cast-Ons 168
Increases 169
Decreases 171
Bind Offs 173
Short-Row Wrap & Turn 174
Kitchener Stitch 176
Joining in the Round 178
Blocking 179
Seaming 180
Embroidery Stitches 183

Index 184

You Really Can Knit It All

Have you ever looked at a pattern, would have loved to proudly declare "I knitted this," but just didn't feel like you had what it took to actually make it? You are not alone. Many knitters turn away from patterns they adore because they feel their knitting skills are inadequate. Every knitter has felt that way at one point or another. But this book is here to tell you that **you can knit it all.**

Within these pages, you will find 65 patterns from *Knit Simple* magazine, a publication known for producing patterns that are fun to knit, beautiful, and accessible to newer knitters. You don't have to be stuck making an endless array of garter stitch scarves (unless that's a real passion for you, in which case, go for it!). You can knit mittens. You can knit hats. You can knit stunning shawls. You can knit cardigans and sweaters. You can knit it all!

Many easy or beginner-friendly patterns might look boring or be boring to knit, but the patterns in this collection were carefully selected to avoid those issues. Who says you can't knit lace? Start with a simple lace pattern in a pair of fingerless mitts. Who says you can't make a blanket? Knit one with an easy ridged chevron pattern and bright colors so the stitches fly by and are beautiful at the same time. What about sweaters and cardigans? Those chosen for this book build off the skills you already have by presenting a variety of constructions that will keep you engaged and get you thinking about knitting in ways you might not have ever imagined. Are these patterns basic or boring? No. Can you really knit them all? Yes.

More than just patterns, this book explains many of the techniques beginners (and beyond!) might find intimidating. Seaming, short-rows, Kitchener stitch, much more are all explained so you can successfully complete them. Sidebars throughout the book offer extra tips and ideas for personalizing your projects (and, yes, you can do that, too!).

When it comes to knitting, the best thing you can do is take the pressure off yourself. Don't worry about what you can't do. Focus on what you want to do. Have patience with yourself. Take your time. If you have to, rip out your work and try again. Knitting isn't a race. It's a journey. It's a talent you will develop one stitch, one technique, one project at a time for the rest of your life.

The possibilities are truly endless with knitting. There's something magical about crafting things with your own two hands. You can express yourself creatively while also being productive, finding yourself with a tangible item as proof of your time and effort. So, don't hold yourself back. You can—and will—knit it all!

How to Use This Book

This book contains many beautiful patterns that you will enjoy making, but before you begin there are some things to consider. This section will help you understand how to make the best use of this book.

HOW TO CHOOSE YARN

Rather than listing the exact yarn that was used to make the samples you see in the photographs in this book, the information about each original yarn has been included. This enables you to find similar yarns, possibly from your stash, to use. When it comes to selecting yarns, some things to consider here are:

THE STANDARD YARN WEIGHT SYSTEM

The Standard Yarn Weight System (seen here) was created by the Craft Yarn Council to help standardize how people refer to various yarn weights, which currently range from 0 (lace) to 7 (jumbo). Every yarn for every pattern of this book includes a classification, appearing as an icon that looks like a skein of yarn with a number inside of it. Referring to these will give you a general idea of what weight (type) of yarn you will need for a pattern. Many yarn companies label their yarns according to these classifications, so you will more often than not find those same skein icons on yarn labels.

SKEIN WEIGHT & YARDAGE

Even if a yarn has a Craft Yarn Council weight classification, there is more to consider. Try your best to match the listed skein weight (often 1¾ or 3½ ounces) and length (yards/meters) of the original yarn to the yarn you will use.

Standard Yarn Weight System

Categories of yarn, gauge ranges, and recommended needle and hook sizes

Yarn Weight Symbol & Category	0 Lace	1 Super Fine	2 Fine	3 Light	4 Medium	5 Bulky	6 Super Bulky	7 Jumbo
Type of Yarns in Category	Fingering 10-count crochet thread	Sock, Fingering, Baby	Sport, Baby	DK, Light Worsted	Worsted, Afghan, Aran	Chunky, Craft, Rug	Super Bulky, Roving	Jumbo, Roving
Knit Gauge Range* in Stockinette Stitch to 4 inches	33–40** sts	27–32 sts	23–26 sts	21–24 sts	16–20 sts	12–15 sts	7–11 sts	6 sts and fewer
Recommended Needle in Metric Size Range	1.5–2.25 mm	2.25–3.25 mm	3.25–3.75 mm	3.75–4.5 mm	4.5–5.5 mm	5.5–8 mm	8–12.75 mm	12.75 mm and larger
Recommended Needle U.S. Size Range	000–1	1 to 3	3 to 5	5 to 7	7 to 9	9 to 11	11 to 17	17 and larger
Crochet Gauge* Ranges in Single Crochet to 4 inch	32–42 double crochets**	21–32 sts	16–20 sts	12–17 sts	11–14 sts	8–11 sts	6–9 sts	5 sts and fewer
Recommended Hook in Metric Size Range	Steel*** 1.6–1.4 mm	2.25–3.5 mm	3.5–4.5 mm	4.5–5.5 mm	5.5–6.5 mm	6.5–9 mm	9–16 mm	16 mm and larger
Recommended Hook U.S. Size Range	Steel*** 6, 7, 8 Regular hook B-1	B-1 to E-4	E-4 to 7	7 to I-9	I-9 to K-10 1/2	K-10 1/2 to M-13	M-13 to Q	Q and larger

* GUIDELINES ONLY: The above reflect the most commonly used gauges and needle or hook sizes for specific yarn categories.

** Lace weight yarns are usually knitted or crocheted on larger needles and hooks to create lacy, openwork patterns. Accordingly, a gauge range is difficult to determine. Always follow the gauge stated in your pattern.

*** Steel crochet hooks are sized differently from regular hooks—the higher the number, the smaller the hook, which is the reverse of regular hook sizing

This Standards & Guidelines booklet and downloadable symbol artwork are available at: **YarnStandards.com**

Beginning on page 168, you will find a section that explains various techniques used throughout the patterns in this book. Some entries include general information about the technique, while others only include step-by-step guidance, often with detailed images. If a pattern uses a specific technique, it will provide the page number where any additional information or how-to guidance can be found.

Be Patient With Yourself

There may be times when you find yourself frustrated. You might drop stitches, end up with too many or too few stitches, have lumpy seams, or end up with an ill-fitting sweater. Many things can go wrong when you work stitch by stitch. But you're not the only one who

> If you are ever unsure about which yarn might work best, ask an experienced knitter or an employee at your local yarn store.

runs into such problems. Even the most experienced knitters make mistakes. Seriously. They do.

So, be patient with yourself. If you get something wrong, see if you can pinpoint where things took a wrong turn and then try again. Don't be afraid of something you haven't done. Try that new technique. One bright side of knitting is that it can usually be undone so you can try again.

So, slow down, take your time, and focus on the positive. Every "mistake" or "set back" is a learning opportunity. Be patient and kind with yourself when things don't go how you expected. You're always learning, and you will get it right. You can knit it all.

ABBREVIATIONS

approx approximately
beg begin(ning)(s)
ch chain
cm centimeter(s)
cn cable needle
cont continu(e)(ing)
dc double crochet
dec decreas(e)(ing)
dec'd decreased
dec'ing decreasing
dpn double-pointed needle(s)
foll follow(ing)(s)
g gram(s)
inc increas(e)(ing)
inc'd increased
inc'ing increasing
k knit
k2tog knit 2 stitches together—1 st dec'd
k3tog knit 3 stitches together—2 sts dec'd
kfb knit into front and back of same stitch
knitwise as if to knit
LH left-hand
lp(s) loop(s)
m meter(s)
M1(L) see page 170
M1R see page 169
M1-p see page 169
m meter(s)
mm millimeter(s)
mos months
oz ounce(s)
p purl
p2tog purl 2 stitches together—1 st dec'd
p3tog purl 3 stitches together—2 sts dec'd
pat(s) pattern(s)

pfb purl into front and back of same stitch—1 st inc'd
pm place maker
psso pass slipped stitch(es) over
rem remain(s)(ing)
rep repeat
RH right-hand
rnd(s) round(s)
RS right side(s)
S2KP slip 2 together knitwise, knit 1, pass slipped sts over knit 1—2 sts dec'd
sc single crochet
SK2P slip 1, knit 2 together, pass slipped stitch over—2 sts dec'd
SKP slip 1, knit 1, pass slipped stitch over—1 st dec'd
sl slip
sl st slip stitch
sm slip marker
ssk (ssp) see page 172
sssk slip 3 knitwise one at a time, knit these 3 stitches together—2 sts dec'd
st(s) stitch(es)
St st Stockinette stitch
tbl through back loop(s)
tog together
WS wrong side(s)
w&t wrap and turn (see page 174)
wyib with yarn in back
wyif with yarn in front
yd yard(s)
yo(s) yarn over(s)

* repeat directions following * as many times as indicated

[ ] repeat directions inside brackets as many times as indicated

LABEL IT

If you need to make additional gauge swatches to get the correct gauge, label each swatch with the project name and needle size you used. This labeling will come in handy if you ever need to refer back to those swatches.

Super Bulky Hat

DESIGNED BY Mari Lynn Patrick

This super bulky hat knits up super quickly with classic ribbing, garter stitch, and simple decreases—all topped, if you wish, with a faux-fur pompom.

MEASUREMENTS
Brim circumference 20"/51cm
Length 8¾"/22.5cm

MATERIALS
- 7oz/200g and 109yd/100m skein of any wool (6)
  1 skein in Off White or Blue
- One size 13 (9mm) circular needle, 16"/40cm long, *or size to obtain gauge*
- One set (5) size 13 (9mm) double-pointed needles (dpn)
- Stitch marker
- Faux-fur pompom (optional)

GAUGE
12½ sts and 19 rnds to 4"/10cm over garter st worked in rnds using size 13 (9mm) needle.
TAKE TIME TO CHECK YOUR GAUGE.

GARTER STITCH
(worked in rnds)
*Purl 1 rnd, knit 1 rnd; rep from * for garter st worked in rnds.

HAT
With circular needle, cast on 44 sts. Join, taking care not to twist sts, and pm for beg of rnd.
Rnds 1–4 *K1, p1; rep from * around.
Dec rnd 5 [K20, SKP] twice—42 sts.

Begin Garter Stitch
*Purl 1 rnd, knit 1 rnd; rep from * 8 times more.
There are 9 garter ridges and the hat measures approx 8"/20.5cm from beg.

Next 4 rnds *K1, p1; rep from * around.

Shape Crown
Note Change to dpn when sts no longer fit comfortably on circular needle.
Dec rnd 1 *K1, p2tog, p1, SKP; rep from * around—28 sts.
Dec rnd 2 Sl 1, [p2tog, SKP] 6 times, p2tog, then SKP last st of rnd tog with first st of rnd and replace beg of rnd marker—14 sts.
Dec rnd 3 [P1, k1] 6 times, p1, SKP last st of rnd tog with first st of rnd and replace beg of rnd marker—13 sts.
Dec rnd 4 [SKP] 6 times, k1—7 sts.
Cut yarn, leaving a long tail. Pull long tail through rem sts and tighten to close crown.

Finishing
Do not block or steam finished hat. If desired, attach faux fur pompom to top of hat using long tail at top.
Weave in ends.

'ROUND AND 'ROUND
Because this hat is knit in the round, the garter stitch pattern is worked as knit one round, purl one round.

Rib Duo Watch Cap

DESIGNED BY Carla Scott

A ribbed and colorful brim, complete with a single contrasting stripe, melts into an even wider ribbing for the crown. Simple color play and textures pair perfectly.

SIZES
Child (Adult Woman, Adult Man). Shown in size Adult Man.

MEASUREMENTS
Brim circumference (slightly stretched)* 14½ (17½, 20)"/37 (44.5, 50.5)cm
Length (with brim rolled) 5½ (7½, 8½)"/14 (19, 21.5)cm
*Will stretch to fit a range of sizes.

MATERIALS
- 1¾oz/50g and 125yd/114m skein of any wool 3
  1 skein each in Orange (A), White (B), and Brown (C)
- One pair each sizes 5 and 6 (3.75 and 4mm) needles, *or size to obtain gauges*

GAUGES
- 26 sts and 30 rows to 4"/10cm over k2, p2 rib (slightly stretched) using smaller needles.
- 24 sts and 28 rows to 4"/10cm over k6, p2 rib (slightly stretched) using larger needles.

TAKE TIME TO CHECK YOUR GAUGES.

K2, P2 RIB
(multiple of 4 sts)
Row 1 (RS) K3, *p2, k2; rep from * to last st, k1.
Row 2 P3, *k2, p2; rep from * to last st, p1.
Rep rows 1 and 2 for k2, p2 rib.

K6, P2 RIB
(multiple of 8 sts)
Row 1 (RS) K3, *p2, k6; rep from * to last 5 sts, p2, k3.
Row 2 P3, *k2, p6; rep from * to last 5 sts, k2, p3.
Rep rows 1 and 2 for k6, p2 rib.

HAT
Brim
With smaller needles and A, cast on 88 (104, 120) sts.
Work in k2, p2 rib for 1 (2, 2)"/2.5 (5, 5)cm, end with a RS row. Cut A.
With B, purl next row on WS. Cont in k2, p2 rib with B for 5 rows. Cut B.
With A, purl next row on WS. Cont in k2, p2 rib with A until piece measures 4½, (5½, 6)"/11.5 (14, 15)cm from beg, end with a RS row. Cut A.

Crown
With C, purl next row (this row is RS of brim and WS of crown).
Change to larger needles.
Beg with a RS row of crown, work in k6, p2 rib for 1½ (2, 2½)"/4 (5, 6.5)cm, end with a WS row.

Shape Crown
Dec row (RS) K3, [p2, k2, k2tog, k2] 10 (12, 14) times, p2, k3—78 (92, 106) sts.
Next row P3, k2, *p5, k2; rep from * to last 3 sts, p3.
Cont in rib as established for 0 (2, 2) rows more.
Dec row K3, [p2, k1, k2tog, k2] 10 (12, 14) times, p2, k3—68 (80, 92) sts.
Next row P3, k2, *p4, k2; rep from * to last 3 sts, p3.
Dec row K3, [p2, k1, k2tog, k1] 10 (12, 14) times, p2, k3—58 (68, 78) sts.
Next row P3, k2, *p3, k2; rep from * to last 3 sts, p3.
Dec row K1, k2tog, [p2, k1, k2tog] 10 (12, 14) times, p2, k2tog, k1—46 (54, 62) sts.
Next row *P2, k2; rep from * to last 2 sts, p2.
Dec row [K2, p2tog] 11 (13, 15) times, k2—35 (41, 47) sts.
Dec row [P2tog, k1] 11 (13, 15) times, p2—24 (28, 32) sts.
Dec row [K2tog] 12 (14, 16) times—12 (14, 16) sts.
Next row (WS) [P2tog] 6 (7, 8) times.
Cut yarn, pull tail through rem sts, and tighten to close crown.

Finishing
With WS facing and beg at cast-on edge, use mattress st over rev St st (see page 182) to sew the first 3½ (4, 4½)"/9 (10, 11.5) cm of back seam.
With RS facing, sew rest of back seam to crown using mattress st over St st (see page 182).
Weave in ends. Steam block lightly, if desired.
Fold brim up to RS.

SEAMS EASY
Mattress stitch is nearly invisible if worked on the right side. Given that the brim of this hat is folded up so the wrong side of it shows, seam the brim on the wrong side and the rest of the hat on the right side.

Staggered Rib Hat

DESIGNED BY Lisa Craig

Bring a bright note to a cold winter day. Worked in the round from the lower edge to the top, this ultra-warm cap shapes up in a totally textural pattern made up of easy knit and purl combinations.

SIZES
Child.

MEASUREMENTS
Brim circumference 17 ½"/44.5cm
Length 8¼"/21cm

MATERIALS
- 3½oz/100g and 100yd/91m skein of any alpaca/wool blend
  1 skein in Pink
- One each sizes 8 and 9 (5 and 5.5mm) circular needle, 16"/40cm long, *or size to obtain gauge*
- One set (4) size 9 (5.5mm) double-pointed needles (dpn)
- Stitch markers

GAUGE
16 sts and 22 rnds to 4"/10cm over pat st using larger needles.
TAKE TIME TO CHECK YOUR GAUGE.

PATTERN STITCH
(multiple of 5 sts)
Rnds 1–4 *P1, k1, p3; rep from * around.
Rnds 5–8 *K1, p1, k1, p2; rep from * around.
Rep rnds 1–8 for pat st.

HAT
With smaller circular needle, cast on 70 sts. Join, taking care not to twist sts, and pm for beg of rnd.
Rnds 1–4 *K1, p1; rep from * around.
Knit 1 rnd, purl 1 rnd.

Begin Pattern Stitch
Change to larger circular needle.
Work rnds 1–8 of pat st 4 times.

Shape Crown
Note Change to dpn when sts no longer fit comfortably on circular needle.
Dec rnd 1 *P1, k1, p1, p2tog; rep from * around—56 sts.
Rnd 2 *P1, k1, p2; rep from * around.
Dec rnd 3 *P1, k1, p2tog; rep from * around—42 sts.
Rnd 4 *P1, k1 p1; rep from * around.
Dec rnd 5 P1, *k1, p2tog; rep from * to last 2 sts, SKP—28 sts.
Rnd 6 *P1, k1; rep from * around.
Rnd 7 *K2tog; rep from * around—14 sts.
Cut yarn, pull tail through rem sts, and tighten to close crown.

Finishing
Weave in ends. Block to measurements.

CUSTOM FIT
For hats with simple stitch patterns worked over a small number of rows/rounds, adjust the fit by working more or fewer repeats than stated. Make this hat more snug by working one 8-round repeat less before shaping the crown.

Twisted Rib Hat

DESIGNED BY Mari Lynn Patrick

A deep turn-back cuff, a contrasting accent color, and twisted rib—worked easily in rows—give this hat extra style and texture.

SIZES
Unisex Small/Medium (Large). Shown in size Small/Medium.

MEASUREMENTS
Brim circumference (unstretched) 18 (19)"/45.5 (48)cm
Length 8¾ (9¼)"/22 (23.5)cm

MATERIALS
- 3½oz/100g and 219yd/200m skein of any wool (4)
  1 skein each Gray (A) and Cream (B)
- One pair size 6 (4mm) needles, *or size to obtain gauge*
- Stitch markers

GAUGE
28 sts and 28 rows to 4"/10cm over twisted k1, p1 rib, slightly stretched, using size 6 (4mm) needles.
TAKE TIME TO CHECK YOUR GAUGE.

STITCH GLOSSARY
twisted SK2P Sl 1 st knitwise tbl, k2tog, pass the sl st over the k2tog.

K1, P1 TWISTED RIB
(over an even number of sts)
Row 1 (RS) P2, *k1 tbl, p1; rep from * to end.
Row 2 (WS) *K1, p1 tbl; rep from * to last 2 sts, k2.
Rep rows 1 and 2 for k1, p1 twisted rib.

HAT
With A, cast on 140 (150) sts.
Work in k1, p1 twisted rib for 14 rows. Cut A.
Next row (RS) With B, p1, k1, *k1 tbl, k1; rep from * to end.
Beg with row 2, cont in k1, p1 twisted rib with B for 3 rows more.
Turning ridge row (RS) Purl.
At this point, RS and WS rows will be reversed for cuff turnback.
Next row (RS) Work row 1 of rib.
Next row (WS) Work row 2 of rib.
Cont in k1, p1 twisted rib pat with B as established for 12 rows more. Cut B.
Next row (RS) With A, p1, k1, *k1 tbl, k1; rep from * to end.
Beg with row 2, cont in k1, p1 twisted rib with A until piece measures 5½ (6)"/14 (15)cm from turning ridge (with cuff folded back).

Shape Crown
Dec row 1 (RS) P2, [pm, twisted SK2P, rib 25 (27)] 4 times, pm, twisted SK2P, rib 23 (25)—10 sts dec'd.
Next row Work even in rib.
Dec row 2 P2, [sm, twisted SK2P, rib to marker] 4 times, sm, twisted SK2P, rib to end—10 sts dec'd.
Next row Work even in rib.
Rep last 2 rows 8 (9) times more—40 sts.
Dec row 3 (RS) P2, [twisted SK2P, p1] 9 times, k1 tbl, p1—22 sts.
Next row Work even in rib.
Dec row 4 P2, [twisted SK2P, p1] 5 times—12 sts.
Cut yarn, leaving long end for seaming. Pull tail through rem sts twice, tighten to close crown, and sew back seam of hat.

Finishing
Weave in ends.

THROUGH THE BACK LOOP (TBL)

To work a stitch through the back loop, knit or purl into the loop that is on the far side of the needle. This twists the stitch and creates a beautiful, compact texture.

Basketweave Hat

DESIGNED BY Carol Sulcoski

A deep textured pattern rings this close-fitting hat. The contrasting crown is worked in panels of stockinette and reverse stockinette.

MEASUREMENTS
Brim circumference 20"/51cm
Length 7"/18cm

MATERIALS
- 1¾oz/50g and 114yd/104m skein of any wool (3) 2 skeins Dark Gray
- One size 5 (3.75mm) circular needle, 16"/40cm long, *or size to obtain gauge*
- One set (5) size 5 (3.75mm) double-pointed needles (dpn)
- Stitch marker

GAUGE
24 sts and 36 rnds to 4"/10cm over basketweave pat using size 5 (3.75mm) needles.
TAKE TIME TO CHECK YOUR GAUGE.

BASKETWEAVE PATTERN
(multiple of 8 sts)
Rnds 1-4 *K4, p4, rep from * around.
Rnds 5-8 *P4, k4, rep from * around.
Rep rnds 1-8 for basketweave pat.

HAT
Cast on 120 sts. Join, taking care not to twist sts, and pm for beg of rnd. Work in basketweave pat until hat measures 4"/10cm from beg, end with a rnd 4 or 8.

BEGIN CROWN
Purl 2 rnds. Knit 1 rnd.
Rib rnd *K14, p6; rep from * around.
Rep rib rnd 6 times more.

Shape Crown
Note Change to dpn when sts no longer fit comfortably on circular needle.
Dec rnd [Ssk, k10, k2tog, p6] 6 times around—108 sts.
Next 5 rnds [K12, p6] 6 times around.
Dec rnd [Ssk, k8, k2tog, p6] 6 times around—96 sts.
Next 4 rnds [K10, p6] 6 times around.
Dec rnd [Ssk, k6, k2tog, ssp, p2, p2tog] 6 times around—72 sts.
Next 3 rnds [K8, p4] 6 times around.
Dec rnd [Ssk, k4, k2tog, p4] 6 times around—60 sts.
Next 2 rnds [K6, p4] 6 times around.
Dec rnd [Ssk, k2, k2tog, ssp, p2tog] 6 times around—36 sts.
Next rnd [K4, p2] 6 times around.
Dec rnd [Ssk, k2tog, p2tog] 6 times around—18 sts.
Dec rnd [K2tog, p1] 6 times around—12 sts.
Dec rnd [K2tog] 6 times around—6 sts.
Cut yarn, pull tail through rem sts, and tighten to close crown.

Finishing
Weave in ends. Block to measurements.

SWITCH IT UP
Not every pattern needs total consistency throughout. The body and crown of this hat are worked in different stitch patterns to create a nice contrast.

Toasty Tot Hat

DESIGNED BY Renée Lorion

Simple stripes in baby's favorite colors make for a cute and quick knit. Pair this with a similarly striped sweater with the colors reversed (see pages 100–102) for an irresistible set.

SIZES
Baby (Toddler, Child). Shown in size Baby.

MEASUREMENTS
HAT
Brim circumference 13½ (17, 18½)"/34.5 (43, 47)cm
Length 6 (7, 7½)"/15 (18, 19)cm

MATERIALS
- 3½oz/100g and 217yd/200m skein of any acrylic/wool/nylon blend (4) 1 skein each in Tan (A) and Blue (B)
- One size 7 (4.5mm) circular needle, 12"/30cm long, *or size to obtain gauge*
- One set (5) size 7 (4.5mm) double-pointed needles (dpn)
- Stitch marker

GAUGE
18 sts and 24 rnds to 4"/10cm over St st using size 7 (4.5mm) needles.
TAKE TIME TO CHECK YOUR GAUGE.

HAT
With circular needle and A, cast on 60 (76, 84) sts. Join, taking care not to twist sts, and pm for beg of rnd.
Rnd 1 *K1, p1; rep from * around.
Rep rnd 1 for k1, p1 rib until piece measures 1"/2.5cm from beg.

Begin Stripe Sequence
Rnds 1 and 2 With A, knit.
Rnds 3–6 With B, knit.
Rnds 7 and 8 With A, knit.
Rnds 9 and 10 With B, knit.

With A only, cont in St st (k every rnd) until piece measures 4 (4¼, 4½)"/10 (11, 11.5)cm from beg.

Shape Crown
Divide sts evenly over 4 dpn—15 (19, 21) sts on each needle.
Dec rnd [K to last 2 sts on needle, k2tog] 4 times around—4 sts dec'd.
Rep dec rnd every rnd 12 (16, 18) times more—2 sts on each dpn, 8 sts total.
Cut yarn, pull tail through rem sts, and tighten to close crown.

Finishing
Weave in ends. Block to measurements.

STRIPE IT UP
For simple striped projects, such as this hat, you can easily change the stripe pattern to match your preferences. Add or remove stripes, adjust their widths, or even add a third color.

Lace Tam

DESIGNED BY Kathy North

A tonal yarn and dainty cat's eye lace pattern give this slouchy topper plenty of bohemian charm. It's knit in the round from the snug ribbed band up.

SIZE
Adult Woman.

MEASUREMENTS
Brim circumference (unstretched) 17"/43cm
Length 8½"/21.5cm

MATERIALS
- 1¾oz/50g and 114yd/100m skein of any merino wool (3) 2 skeins in Tonal Peach
- One each size 6 and 8 (4 and 5mm) circular needle, 16"/40cm long, *or size to obtain gauge*
- One set (5) size 8 (5mm) double-pointed needles (dpn)
- Stitch marker

GAUGE
16 sts and 26 rnds to 4"/10cm over lace pat using larger needle.
TAKE TIME TO CHECK YOUR GAUGE.

LACE PATTERN
(begin with multiple of 4 sts)
Note Beg of rnd moves 1 st to left on rnd 5 and then 1 st to right on rnd 7.
Rnd 1 *K2, [yo] twice, k2; rep from * around.
Rnd 2 *K2tog, k1 into first yo, p1 into 2nd yo, k2tog; rep from * around.
Rnd 3 *K4, [yo] twice; rep from * around.
Rnd 4 *[K2tog] twice, k1 into first yo, p1 into 2nd yo; rep from * around.
Rnd 5 Remove marker, k1, pm, *[yo] twice, k4; rep from * around.
Rnd 6 *K1 into first yo, p1 into 2nd yo, [k2tog] twice; rep from * around.
Rnd 7 Remove marker, pm 1 st to right (last st of previous rnd becomes first st of rnd), k3, [yo] twice, *k4, [yo] twice, rep from * around.
Rnd 8 *[K2tog] twice, k1 into first yo, p1 into 2nd yo; rep from * around.
Rep rnds 5–8 for lace pat.

TAM
With smaller circular needle, loosely cast on 88 sts. Join, taking care not to twist sts, and pm for beg of rnd.
Rnd 1 *K1, p1; rep from * around.
Rep rnd 1 for k1, p1 rib for 9 rnds more.
Next rnd Knit.
Inc rnd *K4, M1; rep from * around—110 sts.
Next rnd Knit.
Inc rnd [K55, M1] twice—112 sts.

Begin Lace Pattern
Change to larger circular needle.
Work in lace pat until piece measures 7½"/19cm from beg, end with a rnd 8.

Shape Crown
Note Change to dpn when sts no longer fit comfortably on circular needle.
Dec rnd 1 [K2tog] twice, *k2, [k2tog] twice; rep from * around—74 sts.
Rnds 2, 4, and 6 Knit.
Dec rnd 3 *K2tog; rep from * around—37 sts.
Dec rnd 5 K1, *k2tog; rep from * around—19 sts.
Dec rnd 7 K1, *k2tog; rep from * around—10 sts.
Cut yarn, pull tail through rem sts, and tighten to close crown.

Finishing
Weave in ends. Block to measurements.

EASY DOES IT

This lace pattern packs a little extra punch with double yarn overs and a shifting beginning of round marker. Take your time and practice until you get the hang of it.

1) Work 2 stitches into the double yarn over as follows: Knit 1 stitch into the first yarn over, as shown. Drop only the first yarn over from the left-hand needle.

2) Bring the yarn to the front, between the needles, and purl into the second yarn over, as shown. Drop the second yarn over from the left-hand needle.

SIZES
Adult Small (Medium/Large). Shown in size Medium/Large.

MEASUREMENTS
Brim circumference (unstretched)
19¾ (22)"/50 (56)cm
Length 8½ (9)"/21.5 (23)cm

MATERIALS
- 1 ¾oz/50g and 93yd/85m skein of any wool (4)
  2 skeins in Blue
- One size 7 (4.5mm) circular needle, 16"/40cm long, *or size to obtain gauge*
- One set (4) size 7 (4.5mm) double-pointed needles (dpn)
- Stitch markers

GAUGE
13 sts and 20 rnds to 4"/10cm over brioche rib, slightly stretched, using size 7 (4.5mm) needles.
TAKE TIME TO CHECK YOUR GAUGE.

STITCH GLOSSARY
Sl 1 k-st with yo Wyif, sl next knit st purlwise to RH needle, wrap yarn over RH needle and around to front again.
Sl 1 p-st with yo Wyif, sl next purl st purlwise to RH needle, wrap yarn over RH needle to back for yarn over, ready to work next knit st.
2-st dec K2tog (next knit st with yo tog with foll purl st), sl k2tog back to LH needle, pass foll knit st with yo on LH needle over st and off needle, sl st back to RH needle—2 sts dec'd.

Brioche Watch Cap
DESIGNED BY Renée Lorion

The deep texture of brioche rib gives the iconic watch cap a fresh update. Wear the cap low for a sleek look or pushed back to create a slouchier silhouette.

WATCH CAP
With circular needle, cast on 64 (72) sts. Join, taking care not to twist sts, and pm for beg of rnd.
Set-up rnd *K1, sl 1 p-st with yo; rep from * around.
Rnd 1 *Sl 1 p-st with yo, k next st and yo tog; rep from * around.
Rnd 2 *P next st and yo tog, sl 1 k-st with yo; rep from * around.
Rep rnds 1 and 2 until cap measures 6½"/16.5cm from beg, end with a rnd 2.

Shape Crown
Note Change to dpn when sts no longer fit comfortably on circular needle.
Place a marker on every 8th (9th) knit rib—4 markers placed.
Dec rnd [Work in pat to knit rib before marked knit rib, work 2-st dec] 4 times—8 sts dec'd.
Cont in pat and rep dec rnd every 4th rnd 2 (3) times more, then every other rnd once—32 sts.
Work 1 rnd even.
Dec rnd [Sl 1 p-st with yo, 2-st dec] 8 times—16 sts.
Cut yarn, pull tail through rem sts, and tighten to close crown.

Finishing
Weave in ends. Block lightly to measurements.

BEGINNER'S BRIOCHE

If you've ever wanted to try brioche knitting, this is the perfect way to get started. Worked in the round with just one color and simple decreases, this hat will help you get the basics down.

Torsades Beret

DESIGNED BY Nitza Coto

This slouchy beret is knit in the round from the ribbed band up. Garter stitch between the traveling cables adds visual interest.

MEASUREMENTS
Brim circumference (slightly stretched) 16"/40.5cm*
Length 9"/23cm
*Ribbed brim will stretch to fit.

MATERIALS
- 1¾oz/50g and 71yd/65m skein of any wool (4)
  2 skeins in Coral
- One each size 7 and 9 (4.5 and 5.5mm) circular needle, 16"/40cm long, *or size to obtain gauge*
- One set (5) size 9 (5.5mm) double-pointed needles (dpn)
- Cable needle (cn)
- Stitch markers

GAUGE
16 sts and 22 rnds to 4"/10cm over St st using larger needle.
TAKE TIME TO CHECK YOUR GAUGE.

STITCH GLOSSARY
6-st RC Sl 3 sts to cn and hold to back, k3, k3 from cn.
8-st RC Sl 4 sts to cn and hold to back, k4, k4 from cn.

BERET
With smaller circular needle, cast on 68 sts. Join, taking care not to twist sts, and pm for beg of rnd.
Rnd 1 *K2, p2; rep from * around.
Rep rnd 1 for k2, p2 rib until piece measures 2"/5cm from beg.
Change to larger circular needle.
Inc rnd [K16, kfb] 4 times—72 sts.
Inc rnd [K1, kfb] 36 times—108 sts.

Begin Cable Pattern
Rnd 1 [K4, p10, k4] 6 times around.
Rnd 2 and all even rnds Knit.
Rnd 3 [K1, M1, k2, ssk, p8, k2tog, k2, M1, k1] 6 times around.
Rnd 5 [K2, M1, k2, ssk, p6, k2tog, k2, M1, k2] 6 times around.
Rnd 7 [K3, M1, k2, ssk, p4, k2tog, k2, M1, k3] 6 times around.
Rnd 9 [K4, M1, k2, ssk, p2, k2tog, k2, M1, k4] 6 times around.
Rnd 11 Knit.
Rnd 13 [K6, 6-st RC, k6] 6 times around.
Rnd 15 Knit.
Rnd 17 [K4, k2tog, k2, M1, p2, M1, k2, ssk, k4] 6 times around.
Rnd 19 [K3, k2tog, k2, M1, p4, M1, k2, ssk, k3] 6 times around.
Rnd 21 [K2, k2tog, k2, M1, p6, M1, k2, ssk, k2] 6 times around.
Rnd 23 [K1, k2tog, k2, M1, p8, M1, k2, ssk, k1] 6 times around.
Rnd 25 [K4, p10, k4] 6 times around.

Shape Crown
Note Change to dpn when sts no longer fit comfortably on circular needle.
Rnd 26 K to last 4 sts, pm for new beg of rnd and remove previous marker.
Rnd 27 [8-st RC, p10] 6 times around.
Rnd 28 Knit.
Dec rnd 29 K7, ssk, p8, k2tog, [k6, ssk, p8, k2tog] 4 times, k6, ssk, p8, pm for new beg of rnd (1 st rem unworked, remove previous marker)—97 sts.
Dec rnd 30 K2tog, k to end of rnd—96 sts.
Rnd 31 [8-st RC, p8] 6 times around.
Rnd 32 Knit.
Dec rnd 33 K7, ssk, p6, k2tog, [k6, ssk, p6, k2tog] 4 times, k6, ssk, p6, pm for new beg of rnd (1 st rem unworked, remove previous marker)—85 sts.
Dec rnd 34 K2tog, k to end to rnd—84 sts.
Rnd 35 [8-st RC, p6] 6 times around.
Rnd 36 Knit.
Dec rnd 37 K7, ssk, p4, k2tog, [k6, ssk, p4, k2tog] 4 times, k6, ssk, p4, pm for new beg of rnd (1 st rem unworked, remove previous marker)—73 sts.
Dec rnd 38 K2tog, k to end of rnd—72 sts.
Rnd 39 [8-st RC, p4] 6 times around.
Rnd 40 Knit.
Dec rnd 41 *[K2tog] 4 times, ssk, k2tog; rep from * around—36 sts.
Dec rnd 42 [K2, k2tog] 9 times—27 sts.
Dec rnd 43 [K2tog] 13 times, k1—14 sts.
Cut yarn, pull tail through rem sts, and tighten to close crown.

Finishing
Weave in ends. Block to measurements.

MARK IT UP

Placing a stitch marker between every repeat can help you stay on track. If you reach a marker and haven't completed the full repeat, you can backtrack and fix your mistake.

Oval Twist Hat & Scarf

DESIGNED BY Jane Yu

No cable needle is required for the mock-cable ribbing on this scarf and hat set. Another perk is that the scarf, which is reversible, features sleek self-finished edges.

MEASUREMENTS

SCARF
Width 7½"/19cm
Length 72"/183cm

HAT
Brim circumference (unstretched)*
16"/40.5cm
Length 8"/20.5cm
*Will stretch to fit a range of sizes.

MATERIALS

- 1¾oz/50g and 87yd/80m skein of any wool (4)
  7 skeins in Blue (Scarf)
  2 skeins in Blue (Hat)
- One pair size 9 (5.5mm) needles, *or size to obtain gauge*
- One size 9 (5.5mm) circular needle, 16"/40cm long
- One set (5) size 9 (5.5mm) double-pointed needles (dpn)
- Stitch marker

GAUGE

25 sts and 24 rows/rnds to 4"/10cm over mock cable pat (slightly stretched) using size 9 (5.5mm) needles.
TAKE TIME TO CHECK YOUR GAUGE.

STITCH GLOSSARY

3-st right twist Skip 2 sts on LH needle, insert needle from front to back into 3rd st on LH needle and k it in front of 2 skipped sts, k 2nd skipped st, k first skipped st, and drop all 3 sts from LH needle.

3-st right twist dec K2tog but do not drop from LH needle, k next st on LH needle then drop all three sts from LH needle—1 st dec'd.

MOCK CABLE PATTERN IN ROWS

(multiple of 5 sts plus 2)
Rows 1 and 3 (RS) P2, *k3, p2; rep from * to end.
Row 2 and all WS rows *K2, p3; rep from * to last 2 sts, k2.
Row 5 P2, *3-st right twist, p2; rep from * to end.
Row 6 Rep row 2.
Rep rows 1–6 for mock cable pat in rows.

MOCK CABLE PATTERN IN ROUNDS

(multiple of 5 sts)
Rnds 1–4 *K3, p2; rep from * around.
Rnd 5 *3-st right twist, p2; rep from * around.
Rnd 6 Rep rnd 1.
Rep rnds 1–6 for mock cable pat in rnds.

SCARF

With straight needles, cast on 47 sts.
Set-up row (WS) *K2, p3; rep from * to last 2 sts, k2.
Rep rows 1–6 of mock cable pat in rows until piece measures approx 72"/183cm from beg, end with a pat row 4. Bind off.

Finishing

Weave in ends. Block lightly to measurements.

HAT

With circular needle, cast on 100 sts. Join, taking care not to twist sts, and pm for beg of rnd.
Rnd 1 *K1 tbl, p1; rep from * around.
Rep rnd 1 for twisted rib for 1¼"/3cm.
Rep rnds 1–6 of mock cable pat in rnds until piece measures approx 6"/15cm from beg, end with a pat rnd 5.

Shape Crown

Note Change to dpn when sts no longer fit comfortably on circular needle.
Dec rnd 1 [K3, p2, k3, p2tog] 10 times—90 sts.
Rnd 2 *K3, p2, k3, p1; rep from * around.
Dec rnd 3 [K3, p2, k2, ssk] 10 times—80 sts.
Rnd 4 *K3, p2, k3; rep from * around.
Dec rnd 5 [K3, p2, 3-st right twist dec] 10 times—70 sts.
Rnd 6 *K3, p2, k2; rep from * around.
Dec rnd 7 [K3, p2, k2tog] 10 times—60 sts.
Dec rnd 8 [K3, p2tog, k1] 10 times—50 sts.
Dec rnd 9 [K2, ssk, k1] 10 times—40 sts.
Dec rnd 10 [K2, ssk] 10 times—30 sts.
Dec rnd 11 [K3tog] 10 times—10 sts.
Cut yarn, pull tail through rem sts, and tighten to close crown.

Finishing

Weave in ends. Block lightly to measurements.

SAME PATTERN, TWO WAYS
Working a pattern in rows will be different than working it in the round. This hat and scarf set is a prime example. Take care to work the correct version of the stitch pattern for each item.

Accordion Rib Hat & Mitts

DESIGNED BY Mari Lynn Patrick

Alternating bands of stockinette stitch and garter stitch give the fabric of these accessories a bouncy stretch similar to an accordion.

MEASUREMENTS
HAT
Brim circumference 21"/53cm
Length 9"/23cm
MITTS
Hand circumference 7½"/19cm
Length 8"/20.5cm

MATERIALS
- 3½oz/100g and 140yd/128m skein of any merino superwash/acrylic/nylon blend
  2 skeins in Gray (A)
  1 skein in Orange (B), Pink (C), and Red (D)
- One each size 6 and 8 (4 and 5mm) circular needle, each 16"/40cm long, *or size to obtain gauge*
- One set (4) each size 6 and 8 (4 and 5mm) double-pointed needles (dpn)
- Stitch markers
- Scrap yarn

GAUGE
17 sts and 26 rnds to 4"/10cm over ridge stripe pat using larger needle.
TAKE TIME TO CHECK YOUR GAUGE.

RIDGE STRIPE PATTERN
With A, knit 1 rnd, *purl 4 rnds.
With B, knit 3 rnds.
With A, knit 1 rnd, purl 4 rnds.
With C, knit 3 rnds.
With A, knit 1 rnd, purl 4 rnds.
With D, knit 3 rnds.
Rep these 24 rnds for ridge stripe pat.

HAT
With smaller circular needle and A, cast on 82 sts. Join, taking care not to twist sts, pm for beg of rnd.
Rnd 1 *K1, p1; rep from * around.
Rep rnd 1 for k1, p1 rib for 5 rnds more. Change to larger circular needle.
Dec rnd K2, [kfb, k9] 8 times—90 sts.
Beg at * (first set of purl 4 rnds), work 23 rnds of ridge stripe pat.
Next, work all 24 rnds of ridge stripe pat.
With A, knit 1 rnd, purl 4 rnds.
Piece measures approx 8"/20.5cm from beg.

Shape Crown
Note Change to dpn when sts no longer fit comfortably on circular needle.
Dec rnd 1 With B, [k2tog, k14, SKP] 5 times—80 sts.
Rnd 2 With B, knit.
Dec rnd 3 With B, [k2tog, k12, SKP] 5 times—70 sts. Cut B.
Rnd 4 With A, knit.
Dec rnd 5 With A, [p2tog, p10, p2tog tbl] 5 times—60 sts.
Rnd 6 With A, purl.
Dec rnd 7 With A, [p2tog, p8, p2tog tbl] 5 times—50 sts.
Rnd 8 With A, purl.
Dec rnd 9 Join C and [k2tog, k6, SKP] 5 times—40 sts.
Rnd 10 With C, knit.
Dec rnd 11 With C, [k2tog, k4, SKP] 5 times—30 sts. Cut C.
Rnd 12 With A, knit.
Dec rnd 13 With A, [p2tog, p2, p2tog tbl] 5 times—20 sts.
Rnd 14 With A, purl.
Dec rnd 15 With A, [p2tog] 10 times—10 sts.
Dec rnd 16 [P2tog] 5 times.
Cut A, pull tail through rem sts, and tighten to close crown.

Finishing
Weave in ends.

DPN & MARKERS

When working in the round on double-pointed needles and the round starts at the beginning of a needle, place a removable (locking) stitch marker onto the first stitch of the round. You can either leave the marker there or move it up every few rounds.

MITTS

Left Hand

With smaller dpn and A, cast on 34 sts with 12 sts on dpn 1 and 11 sts each on dpn 2 and dpn 3. Join, taking care not to twist sts, and pm for beg of rnd.
Rnd 1 *K1, p1; rep from * around.
Rep rnd 1 for k1, p1 rib for 10 rnds more.

BEGIN PATTERN STITCH

Change to larger dpn.
Dec rnd 1 With A, on dpn 1, k10, k2tog; on dpn 2 and dpn 3, knit—33 sts.
Rnds 2-5 With A, purl.
Rnds 6-8 With B, knit.
Rnd 9 With A, knit.
Rnds 10-13 With A, purl.
Rnds 14 and 15 With C, knit.

SHAPE THUMB GUSSET

Inc rnd 16 With C, on dpn 1, k4, pm, M1, k3, M1, pm, k4; on dpn 2 and dpn 3, knit.
Rnd 17 With A, knit.
Inc rnd 18 With A, on dpn 1, p4, sm, M1 p-st, p to 1 st before marker, M1 p-st, sm, p4; on dpn 2 and dpn 3, purl.
Rnd 19 With A, purl.
Inc rnd 20 With A, rep inc rnd 18.
Rnd 21 With A, purl.
Rnd 22 With D, knit.
Inc rnd 23 With D, on dpn 1, k4, sm, M1, k to marker, M1, sm, k4; on dpn 2 and dpn 3, knit—11 sts between thumb markers.
Rnd 24 With D, k5, sl next 9 sts on scrap yarn for thumb, turn to WS, cast on 3 sts, turn to RS, k to end of rnd—35 sts.
Next rnd With A, knit.
Change to smaller dpn.
Dec rnd With A, k2tog, p1, *k1, p1; rep from * around—34 sts.
Cont in k1, p1 rib for 4 rnds more. Bind off in rib.

THUMB

Return to 9 sts on hold for thumb and with D, pick up and k 5 sts in the 3 cast-on sts and divide these 14 sts over 3 dpn. Work in rnds of k1, p1 rib for 2 rnds. Bind off in rib.

Right Hand

Cast on as for left hand, only with 11 sts on dpn 1 and 2 and 12 sts on dpn 3. Work same as for left hand to shape thumb gusset.

SHAPE THUMB GUSSET

Inc rnd 16 With C, on dpn 1 and dpn 2, knit; on dpn 3, k4, pm, M1, k3, M1, pm, k4

Work rem of right hand same as for left hand but with all shaping for thumb on dpn 3 instead of dpn 1.

Finishing

Weave in ends.

Classic Mittens

DESIGNED BY Rachel Maurer

Simple stockinette mittens are perfect for showing off a single beautiful yarn. If you want more color, work the ribbing in a second color or even add a stripe pattern of your own.

SIZE
Adult Woman.

MEASUREMENTS
Hand circumference 8"/20.5cm
Length 7"/18cm

MATERIALS
- 1 ¾oz/50g and 110yd/100m skein of any baby alpaca (3) 2 skeins in Green
- One set (5) each size 3 and 4 (3.25 and 3.5mm) double-pointed needles (dpn), *or size to obtain gauge*
- Stitch markers
- Stitch holders

GAUGE
20 sts and 30 rnds to 4"/10cm over St st using larger needles.
TAKE TIME TO CHECK YOUR GAUGE.

MITTENS
Right Mitten
With smaller dpn, cast on 40 sts and divide sts evenly over 4 needles (10 sts on each needle). Join, taking care not to twist sts, and pm for beg of rnd.
Rnd 1 *K2, p2; rep from * around.
Rep rnd 1 for k2, p2 rib for 2½"/6.5cm. Change to larger dpn.

THUMB GUSSET
Rnd 1 Knit.
Inc rnd 2 K2, pm (thumb marker), M1R, pm (thumb marker), k to end—41 sts.
Rnd 3 Knit.
Inc rnd 4 K2, sm, M1R, k to marker, M1L, sm, k to end—2 sts inc'd.
Rnds 5 and 6 Knit.
Rep rnds 4-6 five times more—53 sts total, 13 between thumb markers.
Next rnd K2, place next 13 sts for thumb on st holder, remove thumb markers, k18, pm, k to end—40 sts.
Cont in St st (k every rnd) until piece measures 7½"/19cm from beg.

SHAPE TOP
Dec rnd 1 [K2, ssk, k to 4 sts before marker, k2tog, k2, sm] twice—4 sts dec'd.
Rnds 2 and 3 Knit.
Rep rnds 1-3 once, then rep rnds 1 and 2 three times—20 sts.
Rep rnd 1 twice—12 sts.
Place 6 front sts on one needle and 6 back sts on a 2nd needle.
Cut yarn, leaving a long tail. Using Kitchener st, graft rem sts (see page 176).

THUMB
With larger dpn, pick up and k 2 sts along hand edge, pm, k13 thumb sts from holder, pick up and k 3 sts from hand edge, k to marker—18 sts.
Divide sts evenly over 3 needles (6 sts on each needle) and pm for beg of rnd.
Dec rnd 1 K1, ssk, k to last 3 sts, k2tog, k1—16 sts.
Work in St st until thumb measures 1½"/4cm.
Dec rnd [K2tog] 8 times—8 sts.
Next rnd Knit.
Dec rnd [K2tog] 4 times—4 sts.
Cut yarn, pull tail through rem sts, and tighten to close.

Left Mitten
Work as for right mitten to thumb gusset.

THUMB GUSSET
Rnd 1 Knit.
Inc rnd 2 K18, pm (thumb marker), M1R, pm (thumb marker), k to end—41 sts.
Rnd 3 Knit.
Inc rnd 4 K18, sm, M1R, k to marker, M1L, sm, k to end—2 sts inc'd.
Rnds 5 and 6 Knit.
Rep rnds 4-6 five times more—53 sts total, 13 between markers.
Next rnd K18, place next 13 sts for thumb on st holder, remove thumb markers, k2, pm, k to end—40 sts.
Complete same as for right mitten.

FINISHING
Weave in ends. Block lightly to measurements.

AVOIDING GAPS
Picking up stitches may tug on the fabric in ways that create unsightly gaps. If a gap appears, undo the stitch causing it and pick up again in a slightly different area.

SIZE
Adult Woman.

MEASUREMENTS
- Hand circumference 8"/20.5cm
- Length 7½"/19cm

MATERIALS
3½oz/100g balls, each approx 224yd/205m (merino wool)
- 1 ball each in blue (A) and red (B)
- One set (5) each sizes 2 and 3 (2.75 and 3.25mm) double-pointed needles (dpn) *or size to obtain gauge*
- One pair size 3 (3.25mm) needles for working the heart motif back and forth in rows
- Stitch markers
- Stitch holders

GAUGE
22 sts and 32 rnds/rows to 4"/10cm over St st using larger needles.
TAKE TIME TO CHECK YOUR GAUGE.

STITCH GLOSSARY
M1R (see page 169)
M1L (see page 170)
M1 p-st Insert needle from front to back under the strand between the last st worked and the next st on the LH needle. Purl into the back loop to twist the st.

NOTES
1) Mittens are worked in the round to the heart motif, then worked back and forth while knitting the 18 rows of the heart motif, then rejoined and worked in the round to the end of the mitten.
2) When working the heart motif, use separate balls of A on each side of the motif. Do not carry A across back of work. When changing colors, twist yarns on WS to prevent holes in work.

Heart-Motif Mittens

DESIGNED BY Rachel Maurer

You'll fall for these colorful mittens, which sport intarsia-knit hearts at the back of each hand.

Right Mitten
With smaller dpn and B, cast on 44 sts. Divide sts evenly over 4 needles (11 sts on each needle). Join, taking care not to twist sts, and place marker (pm) for beg of rnd.
With A, knit 1 rnd.
Cont with A, work as foll:
Rnd 2 *K2, p2; rep from * around.
Rep rnd 2 for k2, p2 rib for 2½"/6.5cm.
Change to larger dpn.

BEG THUMB GUSSET
Rnd 1 Knit.
Rnd 2 K11, M1R, k11, pm, M1R, pm, k to end— 46 sts.
Rnd 3 Knit.
Rnd 4 Knit to marker, sl marker, M1R, work to marker, M1L, sl marker, knit to end—2 sts inc'd.
Rnds 5 and 6 Knit.
Rep rnds 4-6 five times more—58 sts, 13 between markers.
Next rnd K to marker, place 13 sts for thumb on st holder or scrap yarn, pm, k to end—45 sts.

BEG CHART
Note Chart is worked in St st.
Change to straight needles and work next 18 rows back and forth as foll:
Row 1 (RS) Work chart over 23 sts as foll: With A, k11, join B and k1, sl marker, join a separate ball of, A and k to end.
Row 2 (WS) With A, purl to marker, sl marker, work chart to end.
Cont to work chart in this way through row 18. Cut B and 2nd ball of A.

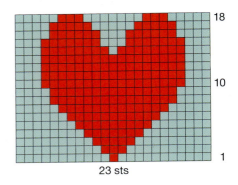

23 sts

Divide sts again over 4 needles and join to work in rounds with A only to end of mitten as foll:
Knit 2 rnds.

SHAPE TOP
Rnd 1 (dec) [K2, ssk, k to 4 sts before marker, k2tog, k2] twice—4 sts dec'd.
Rnds 2 and 3 Knit.
Rep rnd 1-3 once more, then rep rnds 1 and 2 only 3 times more—25 sts.
Next rnd (dec) K2, ssk, k1, k2tog, k2, k2tog, k4, ssk, k4, k2tog, k2—20 sts.
Next rnd (dec) [K2, ssk, k2, k2tog, k2] twice— 16 sts.
Next rnd (dec) [K2, ssk, k2tog, k2] twice—12 sts.
Place 6 front sts on one needle and 6 back sts on a 2nd needle.
Cut yarn leaving a long tail and graft rem sts closed using kitchener st.

Thumb
With larger dpn and A, pick up and k 2 sts along hand edge, knit 13 thumb sts, pick up and k 3 sts from hand edge—18 sts.
Divide sts evenly over 3 needles (6 sts on

each needle).
Knit 1 rnd.
Next rnd (dec) K1, ssk, k to last 3 sts, k2tog, k1—16 sts.
Work even in St st until thumb measures 1½"/4cm, end with a WS row.
Next rnd [K2tog] 8 times—8 sts.
Next rnd Knit.
Next rnd [K2tog] 4 times—4 sts.
Cut yarn and pull through rem sts, draw up and secure. Use tail to sew thumb seam. Sew side seam. Block lightly to measurements.

Left Mitten

Work as for right mitten to thumb gusset

BEG THUMB GUSSET

Rnd 1 Knit.
Rnd 2 K22, pm, M1R, pm, k11, M1R, k11—46 sts.
Rnd 3 Knit.
Rnd 4 Work to marker, sl marker, M1R, work to marker, M1L, sl marker, work to end—2 sts inc'd.
Rnds 5 and 6 Knit.
Rep rnds 4-6 five times more—58 sts, 13 between markers.
Next rnd K to marker, place 13 sts for thumb on st holder or scrap yarn, pm, k to end—45 sts.

BEG CHART

Note Chart is worked in St st.
Change to straight needles and work next 18 rows back and forth as foll:
Row 1 K to marker, sl marker, work chart over 23 sts, using 2 separate balls of A. Complete as for right mitten.

Shell Rib Wristers

DESIGNED BY Annabelle Speer

Easily worked in rows before seaming the side edges together, these hand warmers feature a simple yet eye-catching stitch pattern.

MEASUREMENTS
Circumference (unstretched)
6"/15cm*
Length 9"/23cm
*Will stretch to fit a range of sizes.

MATERIALS
- 1¾oz/50g and 114yd/104m skein of any wool
  2 skeins in Blue
- One pair size 6 (4mm) needles, *or size to obtain gauge*

GAUGE
21 sts and 30 rows to 4"/10cm over shell rib using size 6 (4mm) needles.
TAKE TIME TO CHECK YOUR GAUGE.

SHELL RIB
(beg with multiple of 7 sts plus 2)
Row 1 (WS) P2, *k1, [yo, k1] 4 times, p2; rep from * to end—multiple is now 11 sts plus 2.
Row 2 (RS) K2, *p1, [k1, p1] 4 times, k2; rep from* to end.
Row 3 P2, *k1, p1, ssk, k1, k2tog, p1, k1, p2; rep from * to end.
Row 4 K2, *p1, k1, p3tog, k1, p1, k2; rep from * to end—multiple is back to 7 sts plus 2.
Rep rows 1–4 for shell rib.

WRISTER (make 2)
Cast on 30 sts. Work in shell rib for 9"/23cm, end with a pat row 4. Bind off loosely.

Finishing
Fold wrister in half lengthwise. Beg at lower edge, use mattress stitch on St st (see page 181) to sew side seam for 6½"/16.5cm, leave next 1"/2.5cm unsewn for thumb opening, and use mattress stitch on St st to sew rem 1 ½"/4cm to close wrister.

SAVING SPACE
The shell rib pattern of these wristers cleverly has 2 stitches of Stockinette stitch at each edge of the pattern, giving you stitches that can easily be seamed together.

Fingerless Mitts

DESIGNED BY Jim Cox

Knit mostly in the round, these finger-freeing mitts sandwich chunky k4, p1 ribbing between skinny k1, p1 ribbing for a snug (and stylish) fit.

MEASUREMENTS
Hand circumference 8"/20.5cm
Length (with rib folded) 9"/23cm

MATERIALS
- 1¾oz/50g and 110yd/100m skeins of any baby alpaca 2 skeins in Navy
- One set (5) size 3 (3.25mm) double-pointed needles (dpn), *or size to obtain gauge*
- Stitch marker

GAUGE
25 sts and 30 rnds to 4"/10cm over k4, p1 rib using size 3 (3.25mm) needles. *TAKE TIME TO CHECK YOUR GAUGE.*

MITT (MAKE 2)
Cast on 50 sts and divide over 4 dpn. Join, taking care not to twist sts, and pm for beg of rnd.
Rnd 1 *K1, p1; rep from * around.
Rep rnd 1 for k1, p1 rib for 16 rnds more.
Knit 2 rnds.
Rnd 20 K2, p1, *k4, p1; rep from * to last 2 sts, k2.
Rep rnd 20 until piece measures 4½"/11.5cm from beg.
Turn work and cont in rows for thumb opening as foll:
Next row (WS) P1 tbl, work in rib as established to end.
Next row (RS) K1tbl, work in rib as established to end.
Rep last 2 rows for rib for 9 rows more.
Next row (RS) K1 tbl, work in rib to last st, k last st tbl. Do *not* turn work, join and cont in rnds as foll:
Next rnd Rep rnd 20.
Cont in k4, p1 rib as established until piece measures 2½"/6.5cm from thumb opening.
Knit 2 rnds.
Work 17 rnds in k1, p1 rib.
Bind off in rib.

Finishing
Weave in ends.
Fold k1, p1 rib at top to RS to wear.

THUMBS UP
These clever mitts are mostly worked in the round. A small section is worked in rows to create an easy thumb opening. No seaming required!

Sweet Stripes Baby Booties

DESIGNED BY Rosemary Drysdale

These booties are worked in a two-row garter-stitch stripe pattern, beginning at the sole. The straps are a continuation of the heel stitches, each worked in one of the two colors.

SIZES
3-6 months (12 months). Shown in size 3-6 months.

MEASUREMENTS
Sole length 4 (4¾)"/10 (12)cm

MATERIALS
- 3½oz/100g and 220yd/200m skein of any acrylic 1 skein in Green (A) and Blue (B)
- One pair size 5 (3.75mm) needles, *or size to obtain gauge*

GAUGE
24 sts and 48 rows to 4"/10cm over garter st using size 5 (3.75mm) needles. TAKE TIME TO CHECK YOUR GAUGE.

STRIPE PATTERN
2 rows A, 2 rows B.
Rep these 4 rows for stripe pat.

BOOTIE (MAKE 2)
With A, cast on 33 sts for bottom of sole. Work in garter st (k every row) and stripe pat as foll:
Rows 1, 3, 5, and 7 (RS) Knit.
Inc row 2 K1, M1, k15, M1, k1, M1, k15, M1, k1—37 sts.
Inc row 4 K2, M1, k15, M1, k3, M1, k15, M1, k2—41 sts.
Inc row 6 K3, M1, k15, M1, k5, M1, k15, M1, k3—45 sts.
Inc row 8 K4, M1, k15, M1, k7, M1, k15, M1, k4—49 sts.

Size 3-6 Months ONLY
Rows 9-17 Knit.
Dec row 18 K16, [ssk] 4 times, k1, [k2tog] 4 times, k16—41 sts.
Row 19 Knit.

Size 12 Months ONLY
Row 9 Knit.
Inc row 10 K5, M1, k15, M1, k9, M1, k15, M1, k5—53 sts.
Row 11 Knit.
Inc row 12 K6, M1, k15, M1, k11, M1, k15, M1, k6—57 sts.
Rows 13-21 Knit.
Dec row 22 K18, [ssk] 5 times, k1, [k2tog] 5 times, k18—47 sts.
Row 23 Knit.

BOTH SIZES
Row 20 (24) (WS) With B, k10 (12), bind off center 21 (23) sts, k to end—10 (12) sts rem for 1st strap.

First Strap
Cut A and cont with B only as foll:
Row 21 (25) (RS) With B, k10 (12), turn. On these 10 (12) sts only, knit 2 rows.
Row 24 (28) (WS) Using cable cast-on, cast on 12 (14) sts for strap and k22 (26).
Buttonhole row 25 (29) K to last 3 sts, yo, k2tog, k1.
Row 26 (30) Knit. Bind off.

Second Strap
With RS facing, rejoin A to 10 (12) sts on LH needle. Cont with A only as foll:
Row 21 (25) (RS) Knit.
Row 22 Knit.
Row 23 (27) (RS) Using cable cast-on, cast on 10 (12) sts for strap and k22 (26).
Row 24 (28) Knit.
Buttonhole row 25 (29) K1, k2tog, yo, k to end.
Row 26 (30) Knit. Bind off.

Finishing
Fold bootie in half and sew sole and back heel seam. Sew buttons to bootie just below straps.
Weave in ends. Block to measurements.

SHAPING UP
These booties are knit in rows and then folded and seamed along the cast-on edge (for the sole) and side edges (for the heel/back edge). Use your preferred seaming method along each type of edge.

Cabled Baby Booties

DESIGNED BY Jane Herron

A garter-stitch sole progresses into a lace-patterned instep that is repeated on each side of these adorable booties. Chain-stitch ties with pompoms keep the fit snug.

SIZE
6 months.

MEASUREMENTS
Sole length 4"/10cm
Foot circumference 4½"/11.5cm

MATERIALS
- 1¾oz/50g and 218yd/200m skein of any superwash wool/nylon blend (1) 1 skein in Green
- One pair size 1 (2.25mm) needles, *or size to obtain gauge*
- One size B-1 (2.25mm) crochet hook
- Stitch markers
- Small pompom maker

GAUGE
32 sts and 64 rows to 4"/10cm over garter st using size 1 (2.25mm) needles.
TAKE TIME TO CHECK YOUR GAUGE.

LACE PANEL 1
(over 15 sts)
Row 1 (RS) P3, yo, k3, SK2P, k3, yo, p3.
Row 2 and all WS rows Purl.
Row 3 P3, k1, yo, k2, SK2P, k2, yo, k1, p3.
Row 5 P3, k2, yo, k1, SK2P, k1, yo, k2, p3.
Row 7 P3, k3, yo, SK2P, yo, k3, p3.
Row 8 Purl.
Rep rows 1–8 for lace panel 1.

LACE PANEL 2
(over 9 sts)
Row 1 (RS) Yo, k3, SK2P, k3, yo.
Row 2 and all WS rows Purl.
Row 3 K1, yo, k2, SK2P, k2, yo, k1.
Row 5 K2, yo, k1, SK2P, k1, yo, k2.
Row 7 K3, yo, SK2P, yo, k3.
Row 8 Purl.
Rep rows 1–8 for lace panel 2.

BOOTIE (MAKE 2)
Cast on 49 sts.
Row 1 (RS) K1, kfb, k22, yo, k1, yo, k22, kfb, k1—53 sts.
Inc row 2 K1, kfb, k to last 2 sts, kfb, k1—55 sts.
Inc row 3 K1, kfb, k24, pm, yo, k3, yo, pm, k24, kfb, k1—59 sts.
Inc row 4 Rep inc row 2—61 sts.
Row 5 K to marker, sm, yo, k to marker, yo, sm, k to end—2 sts inc'd.
Row 6 Knit.
Rep last 2 rows 5 times more—73 sts total, 17 sts between markers.
Remove markers. Pm to mark center 15 sts, with 29 sts on either side.
Knit 4 rows.

Instep
Dec row 1 (RS) K28, sl 1 wyib, sm, p3, yo, k3, SK2P, k3, yo, p3, sm (row 1 of lace panel 1 has been worked over center 15 sts), SKP, turn.
Cont to work lace panel 1 over center 15 sts and dec sts on either side of center sts as foll:
Dec row 2 (WS) Sl 1 wyif, p15 (for lace panel 1), p2tog, turn.
Dec row 3 (RS) Sl 1, work next row of lace panel 1 over 15 sts, SKP, turn.
Dec rows 4–23 Rep dec rows 2 and 3 ten times.
Dec row 24 Sl 1, p15 (for lace panel 1), p2tog, k to end—49 sts.
Remove center markers.

Leg
Eyelet row (RS) Sl 1, k1, *yo, k2tog; rep from * to last 3 sts, k3.
Next row Sl 1, p to end.
Dec row 1 (RS) Sl 1, k2tog, p1, p2tog, yo, k2, k2tog, SK2P, k2, k2tog, yo, p3, yo, k3, SK2P, k3, yo, p3, yo, k2, k2tog, SK2P, k2, k2tog, yo, p1, p2tog, k2tog, k1—41 sts.
Row 2 Purl.
Row 3 Sl 1, k1, p2, [pm, work row 3 of lace panel 2 over next 9 sts, pm, p3] twice, work row 3 of lace panel 2 over next 9 sts, pm, p2, k2.
Row 4 and all WS rows Purl.
Cont lace panel 2 over sts between markers, and sts outside of markers on RS rows as established in rows 3 and 4, for 20 rows more, end with a pat row 8, and dec 3 sts on last WS row—38 sts.

CROCHET DETAILS
Simple crochet details are commonly added to knitted items. Making crochet chains are a quick and easy way to make the ties for these booties.

Cuff
Row 1 (RS) Sl 1, k1, *p2, k2; rep from * to end.
Row 2 Sl 1, p1, *k2, p2; rep from * to end.
Rep rows 1 and 2 for k2, p2 rib 4 times more.

Bind off loosely in rib. Cut yarn, leaving long tail for sewing.

Finishing
Sew back and foot seam. Weave in ends. With crochet hook, make a 17"/43cm chain. Thread chain through eyelets in eyelet row.
Make two small pompoms and trim down to 1"/2.5cm diameter. Secure a pompom to each end of chain. Tie chain in a bow at front of bootie.

Hedgehog Slippers

DESIGNED BY Pat Olski

The sides, sole, and back of these fanciful footies are worked in garter stitch while contrasting stockinette stitch forms the adorable faces.

SIZES
Toddler (Child). Shown in size Child.

MEASUREMENTS
Foot circumference 5 (6)"/12.5 (15)cm
Foot length 5¾ (7¼)"/14.5 (18.5)cm

MATERIALS
- 3½oz/100g and 191yd/175m skein in any wool (4)
  1 skein each in Brown (A) and Light Brown (B)
- One pair size 6 (4mm) needles, *or size to obtain gauge*
- One set (4) size 6 (4mm) double-pointed needles (dpn)
- Stitch markers
- Stitch holders
- Tapestry needles for French knot

GAUGE
18 sts and 34 rows to 4"/10cm over garter st using size 6 (4mm) needles.
TAKE TIME TO CHECK YOUR GAUGE.

NOTES
1) Heel and foot of slipper are knit flat, then work is joined to work toe in the round.
2) When working garter section, slip the last stitch of every row with yarn in front.

SLIPPER (MAKE 2)
With A, cast on 22 (26) sts, leaving long tail.
Work in garter st (k every row), slipping last st of every row wyif, until piece measures 3½ (5)"/9 (12.5)cm from beg.

Change to dpn as foll:
Next rnd K7 (8) onto first dpn, k7 (8) onto 2nd dpn, k7 (9) onto 3rd dpn, join to work in the rnd by knitting last st tog with first st in rnd—21 (25) sts.
Cut A, leaving long tail.
Join B, knit 1 rnd. Cont with B only.
Dec rnd 1 K2, [k2tog, k3] 3 (4) times, k2tog, k2 (1)—17 (20) sts.
Rnds 2–5 Knit.
Dec rnd 6 K1, [k2tog, k2] 3 (4) times, k2tog, k2 (1)—13 (15) sts.
Rnds 7–9 Knit.
Rnd 10 K1, [k2tog, k1] 3 (4) times, k2tog, k1 (0)—9 (10) sts.
Cut B.

Nose
Join A, knit 2 rnds.
Dec rnd [K2tog] 4 (5) times, k1 (0)—5 sts.
Knit 1 rnd.
Cut yarn, pull tail through rem sts, and tighten to close.

Ears (make 2)
With B, cast on 4 sts.
Row 1 Knit.
Dec row 2 K1, k2tog, k1—3 sts.
Dec row 3 S2KP—1 st.
Cut yarn, leaving long tail for sewing, and pull through last st.

Finishing
Sew ears to first rnd in B approx 5 sts apart.
With A, make French knots (see page 183) for eyes 2 rnds from each ear.
Use tail in A at toe to sew ½ (1)"/1.5 (2.5)cm of foot closed.
Use tail from cast-on to sew back seam.
Weave in ends.

FINISHING TOUCHES

Sometimes adding a few extra pieces or embroidery stitches makes all the difference. Here, the hedgehog really comes to life with those simple extra details.

Color-Tipped Slippers

DESIGNED BY Sandi Prosser

These super simple slippers feature garter stitch heels worked flat followed by stockinette toes worked in the round. Finish them off by "tipping" them in a contrasting color.

SIZES
Adult Small (Medium, Large, X-Large). Shown in size Medium.

MEASUREMENTS
Foot length 9 (9½, 10½, 11)"/23 (24, 26.5, 28)cm

MATERIALS
- 3½oz/100g and 219yd/200m skein of any wool/viscose/nylon blend
  1 skein in Tan Tweed (A)
  Small amount in Red (B)
- One pair size 6 (4mm) needles, *or size to obtain gauge*
- One set (5) size 6 (4mm) double-pointed needles (dpn)
- One size F-5 (3.75mm) crochet hook
- Stitch marker

GAUGE
20 sts and 32 rows/rnds to 4"/10cm over St st using larger needles.
TAKE TIME TO CHECK YOUR GAUGE.

NOTES
1) Slipper is worked in one piece, beginning at the back heel.
2) After heel section has been worked back and forth, foot section is worked in the round to the toe.

SLIPPER (MAKE 2)
Cast on 48 sts. Beg with a RS row, work in garter st (k every row) until piece measures 4½ (4½, 5, 5)"/11.5 (11.5, 12.5, 12.5)cm from beg, end with a WS row.
Joining rnd With first dpn, k12; with 2nd dpn, k12; with 3rd dpn, k12; with 4th dpn, k12.
Join, taking care not to twist sts, and pm for beg of rnd.
Work in St st (k every rnd) until piece measures 3 (3½, 4, 4½"/7.5 (9, 10, 11.5)cm from joining rnd or approx 1½"/4cm less than desired foot length.

SHAPE TOE
Dec rnd 1 On dpn 1, k to last 3 sts, k2tog, k1; on dpn 2, k1, ssk, k to end; on dpn 3, k to last 3 sts, k2tog, k1; on dpn 4, k1, ssk, k to end—4 sts dec'd.

Rnd 2 Knit.
Rep rnds 1 and 2 three times more, then rep rnd 1 only 4 times—16 sts.
Cut yarn, leaving a long tail.
Sl first 4 sts of rnd onto dpn 4.
Sl sts from dpn 2 to dpn 3.
Using Kitchener stitch (see page 176), graft tog 8 sts from each dpn.

Finishing
Fold cast-on edge in half and sew tog for back heel seam.
We ave in ends. Block lightly to measurements.

EDGING
With RS facing, crochet hook and B, beg at back seam, work a single crochet edging evenly around foot opening. Fasten off.

THIS WAY, THAT WAY

These slippers, worked both in rows and in the round, are a prime example of how simple methods can be combined to make something special.

Diamonds Headband

DESIGNED BY Annabelle Speer

This headband is made from one long rectangle with its cast-on and bound-off stitches sewn together. Moss stitch embedded in cabled diamonds makes the pattern pop.

MEASUREMENTS
Width 4½"/11.5cm
Length 20"/51cm

MATERIALS
- 3½oz/100g and 127yd/116m skein of any superwash merino 🔵 1 skein in Blue
- One pair size 10½ (6.5mm) needles, *or size to obtain gauge*
- Cable needle (cn)
- Stitch markers

GAUGE
22 sts and 32 rows to 4"/10cm over St st using size 10½ (6.5mm) needles.
TAKE TIME TO CHECK YOUR GAUGE.

STITCH GLOSSARY
3-st RPC Sl 1 st to cn and hold to *back*, k2, p1 from cn.
3-st LPC Sl 2 sts to cn and hold to *front*, p1, k2 from cn.
5-st LPC Sl 3 sts to cn and hold to *front*, k2, sl the p st from cn to LH needle and p it, k2 from cn.

NOTE
When following the chart, read RS (odd-numbererd) rows from right to left and WS (even-numbered) rows from left to right.

SEED STITCH
(even number of sts)
Row 1 (RS) *K1, p1; rep from * to end.
Row 2 P the knit sts and k the purl sts.
Rep rows 1 and 2 for seed st.

HEADBAND
Cast on 19 sts.
Set-up row 1 (RS) K1, p1, pm, k3, [k1, p1] 4 times, k1, k3, pm, k1, p1.
Set-up row 2 P1, k1, sm, p4, [k1, p1] 4 times, p3, sm, p1, k1.

Begin Patterns
Row 1 (RS) Work 2 sts in seed st, sm, work row 1 of chart over 15 sts, sm, work 2 sts in seed st.
Row 2 Work 2 sts in seed st, sm, work next row of chart over 15 sts, sm, work 2 sts in seed st.
Cont in pats as established until rows 1–22 of chart have been worked 5 times.
Next row (RS) Work 2 sts in seed st, sm, k3, [p1, k1] 5 times, k2, sm, work 2 sts in seed st.
Next row Work 2 sts in seed st, sm, p3, [k1, p1] 5 times, p2, sm, work 2 sts in seed st.
Bind off.

Finishing
Sew bound-off edge to cast-on edge. Weave in ends. Block lightly to measurements.

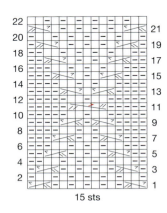

15 sts

STITCH KEY
☐ k on RS, p on WS
⊟ p on RS, k on WS
▱ 3-st RPC
▱ 3-st LPC
▱ 5-st LPC

LAYING FLAT
Some knitted fabrics naturally curl in on themselves. Two simple seed stitches at each end of the rows of this headband help to reduce curling. Blocking can also help.

Planted Headband

DESIGNED BY Audrey Drysdale

Worked widthwise back and forth in rows, this sleek headband is all in seeded rib, with the center section shaped by short-rows. The two side edges are seamed at the back.

MEASUREMENTS
Circumference 17"/43cm*
Length (at longest point) 5"/13cm
*Will stretch to fit a range of sizes.

MATERIALS
- 5.29oz/150g and 218yd/199m skein of any alpaca/wool blend 1 skein Blue
- One pair size 6 (4mm) needles, *or size to obtain gauge*
- Removable stitch markers

GAUGE
22 sts and 30 rows to 4"/10cm over seeded rib pat (slightly stretched) using size 6 (4mm) needles.
TAKE TIME TO CHECK YOUR GAUGE.

SEEDED RIB PATTERN
(multiple of 4 sts plus 3)
Row 1 *K2, p2; rep from * to last 3 sts, k2, p1.
Rep row 1 for seeded rib pat.

HEADBAND
With size 6 (4mm) needles, cast on 95 sts.
Beg with a RS row, work in seeded rib pat for 6 rows.

Shape Headband
Row 1 (RS) Work pat over 86 sts, w&t (see page 174), pm on wrapped st.
Row 2 (WS) Work pat over 77 sts, w&t, pm on wrapped st.
Row 3 Work pat to 6 sts before marker, w&t, move marker onto last wrapped st. Rep last row 9 times more—17 sts rem between marked sts.

Note In following section, pick up the wrapped sts as you work over them. You will turn to create additional short-rows, but you will not wrap sts here—simply turn your work and continue.
Note The column of knit stitches on each side begins the k2, p2 seeded rib pattern repeat.
Row 1 (RS) Work pat across 23 sts. Turn.
Row 2 Work pat across 29 sts. Turn.
Row 3 Work pat across 35 sts. Turn.
Cont as established, working 6 more sts in pat at end of each row until all sts have been worked in pat.
Work 6 rows in pat across all sts. Bind off in pat.

Finishing
Sew side edges of headband tog for center back seam.
Weave in ends.

STAYING IN PATTERN

"Work pat" or "Cont in pat" means to proceed knitting in a way so that the stitch pattern remains continuous. Noting where repeats begin will help you know where to pick up the stitch pattern and how to continue it.

Diagonal Ridge Shawl

DESIGNED BY Anastasia Blaes

Purl-ridge patterns give this shawl a graphic look. After the center chevron panel is complete, the side panels are picked up from either edge and shaped with decreases to the outer points.

MEASUREMENTS
Width (upper edge) 50"/127cm
Length (center) 34"/86.5cm

MATERIALS
- 3½oz/100g and 127yd/116m skein of any superwash wool (5)
  5 skeins in Yellow
- One size 10 (6mm) circular needle, 40"/100cm long, *or size to obtain gauge*

GAUGE
14 sts and 24 rows to 4"/10cm over chevron and ridge patterns using size 10 (6mm) needles.
TAKE TIME TO CHECK YOUR GAUGE.

NOTES
1) Shawl uses all 5 skeins. It may be necessary to unravel and use your gauge swatch.
2) Circular needle is used to accommodate the large number of stitches. Do not join.

SHAWL
Center Panel
Cast on 45 sts. Knit 1 row.

CHEVRON PATTERN
Row 1 (RS) Kfb, k20, S2KP, k20, kfb.
Row 2 K1, p to last st, k1.
Row 3 Rep row 1.
Ridge row 4 Rep row 1.
Rep rows 1–4 for chevron pat 29 times more. Piece measures approx 34"/86.5cm.

FILL TOP OF CHEVRON
Row 1 (RS) Knit.
Row 2 K1, p to last st, k1.
Row 3 K24, k2tog, k1, turn.
Row 4 Sl 1, p4, p2tog, p1, turn.
Row 5 Sl 1, k5, k2tog, k1, turn.
Row 6 Sl 1, P6, p2tog, p1, turn.
Row 7 Sl 1, k to 1 st before previous turn, k2tog, k1, turn.
Row 8 Sl 1, k to 1 st before previous turn, p2tog, p1, turn.
Rep rows 7 and 8 seven times more—25 sts. Knit 2 rows. Bind off.

Left-Side Triangle
With RS facing, beg at bound-off edge, pick up and k 95 sts along left side of center panel to cast-on edge.
Knit 1 row on WS.

RIDGE PATTERN
Row 1 (RS) K to last 3 sts, ssk, k1.
Row 2 K1, ssp, p to last st, k1.
Row 3 K to last 3 sts, ssk, k1.
Ridge row 4 Knit.
Rep rows 1–4 until 2 sts rem. Bind off.

Right-Side Triangle
With RS facing, beg at cast-on edge, pick up and k 95 sts along right side of center panel to bound-off edge. Knit 1 row on WS.

RIDGE PATTERN
Row 1 (RS) K1, k2tog, k to end.
Row 2 K1, p to last 3 sts, p2tog, k1.
Row 3 K1, k2tog, k to end.
Ridge row 4 Knit.
Rep rows 1–4 until 2 sts rem. Bind off.

Finishing
Weave in ends. Block to measurements.

MOD SQUAD
Modular knitting is a technique where you pick up stitches from a previously made piece and work a new section using those stitches. This shawl uses that method to elevate simple ridge patterns and common decreases.

All Angles Wrap

DESIGNED BY The Knit Simple Design Team

Three looks start with just three cast-on stitches—increases are worked from the V-point to the top. Braided ties provide closure no matter which way you choose to wrap up.

MEASUREMENTS
Width (upper edge) 66"/167.5cm
Length (center) 22"/56cm

MATERIALS
- 3½oz/100g and 98yd/90m skein of any wool
  5 hanks in Variegated Blue
- One size 13 (9mm) circular needle, 40"/100cm long, *or size to obtain gauge*

GAUGE
10 sts and 20 rows to 4"/10cm over garter st using size 13 (9mm) needle.
TAKE TIME TO CHECK YOUR GAUGE.

NOTE
Circular needle is used to accommodate the large number of stitches. Do *not* join.

WRAP
Cast on 3 sts.
Row 1 Knit.
Inc row 2 Kfb, k to last st, kfb—2 sts inc'd.
Rows 3 and 4 Rep row 2.
Rep rows 1-4 for 26 times more—165 sts.
Knit 1 row. Bind off.

Finishing
Weave in ends. Block to measurements.

TIES (MAKE 2)
Holding 3 strands of yarn together for each strand of braid, make a braid 36"/91.5cm long. Tie knot approx 4"/10cm from end of braid and allow ends to unravel to form a tassel. Secure opposite end to side point of shawl.
Rep for 2nd braid, securing to opposite side point.

FUN-CTIONAL TIES
The ties of this triangular shawl are fashionable and practical. You can simply let them dangle or use them to tie the wrap in place however you please to drape it.

Theatre Shawl

DESIGNED BY Vanessa Ewing

This graceful shoulder-skimming shawl begins with a picot edge cast-on before moving on to a strip of segmented lace followed by a garter stitch body shaped with short rows.

MEASUREMENTS
Width (top edge) 54"/137cm
Length (center) 14"/35.5cm

MATERIALS
- 1¾oz/50g skeins and 136yd/124m skein of any merino wool
  4 skeins in Purple
- One each size 5 and 7 (3.75 and 4.5mm) circular needle, 32"/80cm long, *or size to obtain gauge*
- Stitch marker

GAUGE
16 sts and 40 rows to 4"/10cm over garter st using larger needles.
TAKE TIME TO CHECK YOUR GAUGE.

NOTES
1) Shawl is worked from lower edge and shaped with short-rows.
2) Circular needle is used to accommodate the large number of stitches. Do *not* join.
3) When following the chart, read WS (odd-numbererd) rows from left to right and RS (even-numbered) rows from right to left.

SHAWL
With smaller needle, work picot edge cast-on as foll:
*[Cast on 5 sts using knitted cast-on (see page 168), bind off 2 sts, sl 1 st back to LH needle] twice, cast on 10 sts using knitted cast-on (see page 168), bind off 2 sts, sl 1 st back to LH needle (14 sts cast on); rep from * 14 times more—210 sts.
Cast on 5 sts using knitted cast-on, bind off 2 sts, sl 1 st back to LH needle, cast on 2 sts using knitted cast-on—215 sts.
Next 4 rows Sl 1, k to end.

Lace Section
Note Lace section may be worked from chart or written instructions.
Rows 1, 3, and 5 (WS) Sl 1, k1, *k1, p13; rep from * to last 3 sts, k3.
Row 2 (RS) Sl 1, k1, p1, *k3, k2tog, yo, k3, yo, ssk, k3, p1; rep from * to last 2 sts, k2.
Row 4 Sl 1, k1, p1, *k2, k2tog, yo, k5, yo, ssk, k2, p1; rep from * to last 2 sts, k2.
Row 6 Sl 1, k1, p1, *k1, k2tog, yo, k7, yo, ssk, k1, p1; rep from * to last 2 sts, k2.
Row 7 Sl 1, k1, *k1, p5, k3, p5; rep from * to last 3 sts, k3.
Row 8 Sl 1, k1, p1, *k2tog, yo, k3, p3, k3, yo, ssk, p1; rep from * to last 2 sts, k2.
Rep rows 1–8 for lace section twice more.

Garter Body
Change to larger needle.
Inc row 1 (WS) Sl 1, kfb, k to end—216 sts.
Row 2 (RS) Sl 1, k1, *yo, k2tog; rep from * to end.
Row 3 Sl 1, k107, pm, k108.

SHORT-ROW SHAPING
Note It is not necessary to pick up the wraps as you work over them. You may choose to simply knit the stitches, leaving the wraps where they are.
Short-row 1 (RS) Sl 1, k to marker, sm, k2, w&t.
Short-row 2 K to marker, sm, k2, w&t.
Short-row 3 K to 1 st beyond previously wrapped st, w&t.
Rep short-row 3 until all sts have been worked each side of marker. Bind off loosely.

FINISHING
Weave in ends. Block to measurements, pinning out points along cast-on edge.

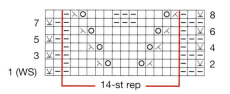

STITCH KEY
- ☐ k on RS, p on WS
- ⊟ p on RS, k on WS
- ⧄ k2tog
- ⧅ ssk
- ○ yo
- ⋎ sl 1 wyib on RS, sl 1 wyif on WS

WRAPS IN GARTER STITCH

Garter stitch hides short-row wraps fairly well, so many knitters do not pick them up as they work over them. Test out each option on a small swatch to see which option you prefer.

Malibu Ripple Shawl

DESIGNED BY Audrey Drysdale

Classic patterns and graphic colors create a totally modern shawl. Knit from the center top edge, it's shaped with yarn overs at the outer edges and center.

MEASUREMENTS
Width (upper edge) 54"/137cm
Length (center) 28"/71cm

MATERIALS
- 3½oz/100g and 220yd/200m skein of any cotton 3 skeins in Variegated Turquoise (A) 1 skein in White (B)
- One size 6 (4mm) circular needle, 32"/80cm long, *or size to obtain gauge*
- Stitch marker

GAUGE
21 sts and 28 rows to 4"/10cm over St st using size 6 (4mm) needle.
TAKE TIME TO CHECK YOUR GAUGE.

NOTE
Circular needle is used to accommodate the large number of stitches. Do *not* join.

SHAWL
With A, cast on 7 sts.
Inc row 1 (RS) K3, yo, k1, yo, k3—9 sts.
Row 2 K3, p to last 3 sts, k3.
Inc row 3 K3, yo, k1, yo, pm, [k1, yo] twice, k3—13 sts.
Row 4 K3, p to last 3 sts, k3.
Inc row 5 K3, yo, k to marker, yo, sm, k1, yo, k to last 3 sts, yo, k3—4 sts inc'd.
Row 6 K3, p to last 3 sts, k3.
Rep Rows 5 and 6 for 12 times more, then rep row 5 once more—69 sts.
Inc row (WS) K3, p1, [M1 p-st, p5] 12 times, p2, k3—81 sts.

Wave Pattern
Note In wave pat, every RS rows increases 4 sts.
Inc row 1 (RS) K3, yo, *[k2tog] 3 times, [k1, yo] 6 times, [k2tog] 3 times; rep from * to 1 st before marker, k1, yo, sm, k1, yo, k1, **[k2tog] 3 times, [yo, k1] 6 times, [k2tog] 3 times; rep from ** to last 3 sts, yo, k3.
Row 2 and all WS rows K3, p to last 3 sts, k3.
Inc row 3 K3, yo, k to marker, yo, sm, k1, yo, k to last 3 sts, yo, k3.
Inc row 5 K3, yo, k2, *[k2tog] 3 times, [k1, yo] 6 times, [k2tog] 3 times; rep from * to 3 sts before marker, k3, yo, sm, k1, yo, k3, **[k2tog] 3 times, [yo, k1] 6 times, [k2tog] 3 times; rep from ** to last 5 sts, k2, yo, k3.
Inc row 7 Rep row 3.
Inc row 9 K3, yo, k4, *[k2tog] 3 times, [k1, yo] 6 times, [k2tog] 3 times; rep from * to 5 sts before marker, k5, yo, sm, k1, yo, k5, **[k2tog] 3 times, [yo, k1] 6 times, [k2tog] 3 times; rep from ** to last 7 sts, k4, yo, k3.
Inc row 11 Rep Inc row 3.
Row 12 Knit. Cut A.
Rows 13-16 With B, rep rows 11 and 12 twice. Cut B.

Inc row 17 With A, rep inc row 3.
Row 18 Rep row 2.
Inc row 19 K3, yo, [k1, yo] 3 times, [k2tog] 6 times, *[k1, yo] 6 times, [k2tog] 6 times; rep from * to 4 sts before marker, [k1, yo] 4 times, sm, k1, [yo, k1] 4 times, [k2tog] 6 times, **[yo, k1] 6 times, [k2tog] 6 times; rep from ** to last 6 sts, [yo, k1] 4 times, k2.
Inc row 21 Rep inc row 3.
Inc row 23 K3, yo, k3, [yo, k1] twice, yo, [k2tog] 6 times, *[k1, yo] 6 times, [k2tog] 6 times; rep from * to 6 sts before marker, [k1, yo] 3 times, k3, yo, sm, k1, yo, k3, [yo, k1] 3 times, [k2tog] 6 times, **[yo, k1] 6 times, [k2tog] 6 times; rep from ** to last 8 sts, [yo, k1] 3 times, k2, yo, k3.
Inc row 25 Rep inc row 3.
Inc row 27 K3, yo, k5, [yo, k1] twice, yo, [k2tog] 6 times, *[k1, yo] 6 times, [k2tog] 6 times; rep from * to 8 sts before marker, [k1, yo] 3 times, k5, yo, sm, k1, yo, k5, [yo, k1] 3 times, [k2tog] 6 times, **[yo, k1] 6 times, [k2tog] 6 times; rep from ** to last 10 sts, [yo, k1] 3 times, k4, yo, k3.
Rows 29-36 Rep rows 11 to 18—153 sts.

Rep rows 1-36 for wave pat twice more. Work rows 1-34 once more (end with a rnd 16 with B) —365 sts.
With B, bind off evenly knitwise.

Finishing
Weave in ends. Block to measurements.

GARTER BORDERS

Placing a few rows or stitches of garter stitch along the edges of a piece creates a tidy edging. This shawl uses garter stitch within the pattern to that effect.

Dipper Shawl

DESIGNED BY Sandi Prosser

This simple yet impactful shawl is worked in garter stitch from the wide top edge to the lower point. An I-cord-like border keeps the edges beautifully tidy.

MEASUREMENTS
Width 21"/53cm
Length 42"/106.5cm

MATERIALS
- 3½oz/100g and 273yd/250m skein of any acrylic/wool blend (3)
  2 skeins in Gray (A)
  1 skein in Sea Green (B)
- One size 6 (4mm) circular needle, 16"/40cm long, *or size to obtain gauge*
- One size G-6 (4mm) crochet hook
- Scrap yarn

GAUGE
22 sts and 44 rows to 4"/10cm over garter st using size 6 (4mm) needle.
TAKE TIME TO CHECK YOUR GAUGE.

SHAWL
With A, cast on 235 sts using provisional cast-on (see page 169).
Rows 1–4 K to last 2 sts, sl last 2 sts wyif.
Dec row 5 K2, ssk, k to last 4 sts, k2tog, sl last 2 sts wyif—2 sts dec'd.
Row 6 K to last 2 sts, sl next 2 sts wyif.
Rep rows 5 and 6 until 81 sts rem.
Cut A and join B.
With B, rep rows 5 and 6 until 7 sts rem.
Dec row (RS) K2, SK2P, sl last 2 sts wyif—5 sts.
Next row K to last 2 sts, sl last 2 sts wyif.
Dec row K1, ssk, sl last 2 sts wyif—4 sts.
Dec row K1, ssk, sl last st wyif—3 sts.
Next row (RS) SK2P. Fasten off.

Finishing
Remove scrap yarn from provisional cast-on, placing cast-on sts onto needle. Join yarn A with RS facing.

I-CORD EDGING
Bind off all sts as foll: Sl 1 wyif, k1, *sl 2 sts back to LH needle, k1, k2tog tbl; rep from * to last 2 sts, sl first st on RH needle over last st, cut yarn and pull through last st.

Weave in ends. Block lightly.

I-CORD EDGES
The slip stitches at the end of each row create an edge similar to the I-cord bind-off that is worked after removing the provisional cast-on. The result is a unified look along all edges.

Peek-a-Boo Lace Shawl

DESIGNED BY Jacob Seifert

A garter tab begins a triangular shawl with alternating bands of stockinette and directional eyelet lace. The entire shawl is edged in garter stitch, ensuring beautiful drape.

MEASUREMENTS
Width (upper edge) 84"/213.5cm
Length (center) 30"/76 cm

MATERIALS
- 3½oz/100g and 188yd/169m skein of any acrylic/nylon/kid mohair/wool/bead/sequin blend (4)
  4 skeins in Purple
- One size 7 (4.5mm) circular needle 40"/100cm long, *or size to obtain gauges*
- Removable stitch markers

GAUGES
- 20 sts and 30 rows to 4"/10cm over St st using size 7 (4.5mm) needles.
- 15 sts and 30 rows to 4"/10cm over either lace pat using size 7 (4.5mm) needles.

TAKE TIME TO CHECK YOUR GAUGES.

NOTE
Move stitch marker up on center stitch as work progresses.

OUTWARD LACE PATTERN
(multiple of 3 sts plus 4)

Inc row 1 (RS) K3, M1R, ssk, yo, *k1, ssk, yo; rep from * to 2 sts before marked st, k2, M1R, k1 (center st), M1L, k2, **yo, k2tog, k1; rep from ** to last 5 sts, yo, k2tog, M1L, k3—4 sts inc'd.

Row 2 and all WS rows K3, p to last 3 sts, k3.

Inc row 3 K3, M1R, *ssk, yo, k1; rep from * to marked st, M1R, k1 (center st), M1L, **k1, yo, k2tog; rep from ** to last 3 sts, M1L, k3—4 sts inc'd.

Inc row 5 K3, M1R, ssk, *yo, k1, ssk; rep from * to marked st, yo, M1R, k1 (center st), M1L, yo, **k2tog, k1, yo; rep from ** to last 5 sts, k2tog, M1L, k3—4 sts inc'd.

Row 6 Rep row 2.

Rep rows 1-6 for outward lace pat.

INWARD LACE PATTERN
(multiple of 3 sts plus 4)

Inc row 1 (RS) K3, M1R, k2, *yo, k2tog, k1; rep from * to last 2 sts before marked st, yo, k2tog, M1R, k1 (center st), M1L, ssk, yo, **k1, ssk, yo; rep from ** to last 5 sts, k2, M1L, k3—4 sts inc'd.

Row 2 and all WS rows K3, p to last 3 sts, k3.

Inc row 3 K3, M1R, *k1, yo, k2tog; rep from * to marked st, M1R, k1 (center st), M1L, **ssk, yo, k1; rep from ** to last 3 sts, M1L, k3—4 sts inc'd.

Inc row 5 K3, M1R, yo, *k2tog, k1, yo; rep from * to last 2 sts before marked st, k2tog, M1R, k1 (center st), M1L, ssk, **yo, k1, ssk; rep from ** to last 3 sts, yo, M1L, k3—4 sts inc'd.

Row 6 Rep row 2.

Rep rows 1-6 for inward lace pat.

SHAWL
Cast on 3 sts. Knit 6 rows.
With RS facing, turn work 90 degrees clockwise, pick up and k 3 sts from side of piece (1 st in each garter ridge), then pick up and k 3 sts from cast-on edge—9 sts.

TIME TO ADJUST
When patterns with varying stitch gauges are worked in the same project sequentially, increase or decrease to the correct number of stitches when changing to the next pattern.

Stockinette Band 1

Set-up row (WS) K3 (selvage sts), k2, pm on last st worked (center st), k1, k3 (selvage sts).
Inc row 1 (RS) K3, M1R, k to marked st, M1R, k1 (marked center st), M1L, k to last 3 sts, M1L, k3—4 sts inc'd.
Row 2 (WS) K3, p to last 3 sts, k3.
Rep rows 1 and 2 fourteen times more, then rep row 1 once more—73 sts.
Dec row (WS) K3, p to last 3 sts, dec'ing 16 sts evenly across to last 3 sts, k3—57 sts.

Lace Band 1

Rep rows 1–6 of outward lace pat twice—81 sts.
Rep rows 1–6 of inward lace pat twice—105 sts.

Stockinette Band 2

Inc row 1 (RS) K3, M1R, [k4, M1] 12 times, k1, M1R, k1 (marked center st), M1L, k1, [M1, k4] 12 times, M1L, k3—28 sts inc'd and 133 sts in total.
Row 2 K3, p to last 3 sts, k3.
Inc row 3 (RS) K3, M1R, k to marked st, M1R, k1 (marked center st), M1L, k to last 3 sts, M1L, k3—4 sts inc'd.
Row 4 K3, p to last 3 sts, k3.
Rep rows 3 and 4 six times, then row 3 once more—161 sts.
Dec row (WS) K3, p to last 3 sts, dec'ing 38 sts evenly across to last 3 sts, k3—123 sts.

Lace Band 2

Rep rows 1–6 of outward lace pat 3 times—159 sts.
Rep rows 1–6 of inward lace pat 3 times—195 sts.

Stockinette Band 3

Inc row 1 (RS) K3, M1R, k2, [M1, k4] 22 times, [M1, k2] twice, M1R, k1 (marked center st), M1L, [k2, M1] twice, [k4, M1] 22 times, k2, M1L, k3—52 sts inc'd and 247 sts in total.
Row 2 K3, p to last 3 sts, k3.
Inc row 3 (RS) K3, M1R, k to marked st, M1R, k1 (marked center st), M1L, k to last 3 sts, M1L, k3—4 sts inc'd.
Row 4 K3, p to last 3 sts, k3.
Rep rows 3 and 4 six times, then row 3 once more—275 sts.
Dec row (WS) K3, p to last 3 sts, dec'ing 68 sts evenly across to last 3 sts, k3—207 sts.

Lace Band 3

Rep rows 1–6 of outward lace pat twice—231 sts.
Rep rows 1–6 of inward lace pat twice—255 sts.

Stockinette Band 4

Inc row 1 (RS) K3, M1R, [k3, M1] 41 times, k1, M1R, k1 (marked center st), M1L, k1, [M1, k3] 41 times, M1L, k3—86 sts inc'd and 341 sts in total.
Row 2 K3, p to last 3 sts, k3.
Inc row 3 (RS) K3, M1R, k to marked st, M1R, k1 (marked center st), M1L, k to last 3 sts, M1L, k3—4 sts inc'd.
Row 4 K3, p to last 3 sts, k3.
Rep rows 3 and 4 six times—365 sts.

BORDER

Inc row 1 (RS) K to center st, M1R, k1 (center st), M1L, k to end—2 sts inc'd.
Row 2 Knit.
Rep rows 1 and 2 twice more—371 sts.
Bind off.

FINISHING

Weave in ends. Steam block into triangular shape and so edges do not curl.

Double Swiss Shawl

DESIGNED BY Holli Yeoh

The shifting of the two pattern stitches—welt and lace—form two smaller triangles inside a larger right-triangle shape.

WELT PATTERN
Work 5 rows in St st (k on RS, p on WS).
Work 3 rows rev St st (p on RS, k on WS).
Rep these 8 rows for welt pat.

LACE PATTERN
(multiple of 3 sts)
Row 1 (RS) *K1, yo, k2tog; rep from * to end.
Row 2 Purl.
Row 3 *K2tog, yo, k1; rep from * to end.
Row 4 Purl.
Rep rows 1–4 for lace pat.

SHAWL
Cast on 129 sts loosely.
Row 1 (RS) *P1, k1; rep from * to last 3 sts, k3.
Row 2 Sl 1, wyif k1 (making yarn over by wrapping yarn over RH needle), k1, *p1, k1; rep from * to end.
Row 3 Sl 1, *k1, p1; rep from * to last 5 sts, k2tog, k1, drop yo, k1.
Row 4 Sl 1, wyif k1, k1, *k1, p1; rep from * to last st, k1.

Lace and Welt Patterns
Row 5 (RS) Sl 1, k2, work row 1 of lace pat over 3 sts, pm, k to last 5 sts, k2tog, k1, drop yo, k1.
Row 6 Sl 1, wyif k1, p to last 3 sts, k3.
Row 7 Work in pats as established to marker, sm, k to last 5 sts, k2tog, k1, drop yo, k1.
Rows 8 and 9 Rep rows 6 and 7.
Row 10 Sl 1, wyif k1, k to 3 sts before

marker, p to last 3 sts, k3.
Row 11 Work in pats to marker, remove marker, cont lace pat over next 3 sts, pm, p to last 5 sts, k2tog, k1, drop yo, k1.
Row 12 Sl 1, wyif k1, k to marker, sm, p to last 3 sts, k3.
Row 13 Work in pats to marker, remove marker, cont lace pat over next 3 sts, pm, k to last 5 sts, k2tog, k1, drop yo, k1.
Rows 14–20 Rep rows 6–12.
Rep rows 13–20 ten times more, then rep rows 13–15 once more—78 sts. Marker will be 3 sts
from end of row, remove marker.
Cont in lace pat only between selvage sts each side.

MEASUREMENTS
Width (shaped edge) 55"/139.5cm
Length (center) 25"/63.5cm

MATERIALS
- 5.3oz/150g and 518yd/473m skein of any cotton/acrylic/other blend (4) 1 skein in Self-striping Earth Tones
- One size 8 (5mm) circular needle, 32"/80cm long, *or size to obtain gauges*
- Stitch markers

GAUGES
- 15 sts and 26 rows to 4"/10cm over welt pat using size 8 (5mm) needle.
- 13 sts and 22 rows to 4"/10cm over lace pat, after blocking, using size 8 (5mm) needle.

TAKE TIME TO CHECK YOUR GAUGE.

NOTES
1) Slip stitches purlwise with yarn in front.
2) Shaping is worked by decreasing 1 stitch at the end of each right side row. For a smooth edge, the first knit stitch following the slipped edge stitch on wrong side rows is worked with the yarn in front, creating a yarn over that is dropped on the next row.
3) The lace pattern is worked before the marker, and the welt pattern after the marker. As the rows are worked, the patterns shift, working more stitches in the lace pattern until the entire row is worked in lace.
4) When shaping into lace pattern, always work a yarn over paired with a decrease and vice versa, otherwise work stitches in Stockinette stitch.
5) Circular needle is used to accommodate the large number of stitches. Do not join.

Row 104 (WS) Sl 1, wyif k1, k1, p to last 3 sts, k3.
Row 105 Sl 1, k2, work in lace pat to last 5 sts, k2tog, k1, drop yo, k1.
Rep last 2 rows until 4 sts rem, end with a RS row.
Next row (WS) Sl 1, k to end.
Next dec row Sl 1, k2tog, k1—3 sts.
Next row Sl 1, k to end.
Next dec row Sl 1, k2tog—2 sts.
Next dec row K2tog. Fasten off last st.

Finishing
Weave in ends.
Block to measurements.

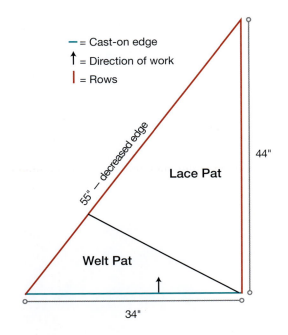

SLIGHT SHIFTS
The incremental shifts in stitch patterns, paired with the decreases along one edge, make it so no change in stitch count is necessary as the patterns transition.

Shifting Tides Scarf

DESIGNED BY Rosemary Drysdale

Work each half of this scarf separately and then seam it together for symmetrical beauty. Use a single yarn in a 5-tone gradient or combine shades of your favorite color(s) to create your own ombré effect.

MEASUREMENTS
Width 7"/18cm
Length 66"/167.5cm

MATERIALS
- 3½oz/100g and 127yd/116m skein of any acrylic/nylon
  2 skeins in a 5-tone White to Blue Ombré OR 1 skein each in 5 colors
- One pair size 10 (8mm) needles, *or size to obtain gauge*
- One extra size 10 (8mm) needle

GAUGE
19 sts and 24 rows to 4"/10cm over ripple pat using size 10 (8mm) needles. *TAKE TIME TO CHECK YOUR GAUGE.*

NOTE
If using an ombré yarn, you may choose to separate the yarn into 5 distinct colors so you can create sharp color changes in the scarf. Otherwise, simply knit and let the shifts happen naturally.

RIPPLE PATTERN
(multiple of 11 sts plus 1)
Row 1 (RS) *K1, yo, k3, k2tog, ssk, k3, yo; rep from * to last st, k1.
Row 2 Purl.
Rows 3–6 Rep rows 1 and 2 twice more.
Row 7 (RS) Purl.
Row 8 Knit.
Rep rows 1–8 for ripple pat.

SCARF
First Half
Cast on 34 sts.
If not using separate colors, work in ripple pat in stripes for 33"/84cm OR work 24 rows in first color, 24 rows in 2nd color, 24 rows in 3rd color, 24 rows in 4th color, 40 rows in 5th color, 16 rows in 4th color, 16 rows in 3rd color, 16 rows in 2nd color, 16 rows in first color. Place sts on a stitch holder.

Second Half
Work same as first half.

Finishing
With 3rd needle, join open sts of each half with 3-needle bind-off (see page 173). Weave in ends. Block to measurements.

PLAYING WITH COLOR
Instead of creating an ombré effect, consider using neutrals with one color that pops, or maybe a handful of neons. Color choice is the easiest way to customize your knitting.

Hound's Tooth Scarf

DESIGNED BY Zahra Jade Knot

A handsome colorwork scarf is simplified by working it in the round.
No worrying about purling or unsightly floats!

MEASUREMENTS
7¼ x 64"/18.5 x 162.5cm

MATERIALS
- 3½oz/100g and 220yd/200m of any wool (4)
  3 skeins each Green (A) and Gray (B)
- One size 7 (4.5mm) circular needle, 16"/40cm long, *or size to obtain gauge*
- Stitch marker

GAUGE
29 sts and 24 rnds to 4"/10cm over St st using size 7 (4.5mm) needle.
TAKE TIME TO CHECK YOUR GAUGE.

SCARF
With A, cast on 104 sts. Join, taking care not to twist sts, and pm for beg of rnd.
Rnd 1 *K2, p2; rep from * around.
Rep rnd 1 for 11 rnds more.
Inc rnd K to last st, M1, k1—105 sts.

Begin Chart
Note Because this scarf is worked in the round, read every row of the chart from right to left. The chart pat is worked in St st (knit every rnd). When changing colors, twist yarns on WS to prevent holes in work. Carry yarn not in use loosley across WS to prevernt puckering.

Rnd 1 (RS) Work 7-st rep 15 times around. Cont to work chart in this way through rnd 8, then rep rnds 1-8 for 45 times more. Cut B.
Dec rnd With A, k to last 2 sts, k2tog—104 sts.
Next rnd *K2, p2; rep from * around.
Rep last rnd 11 times more. Bind off in rib.

Finishing
Weave in ends. Block to measurements.

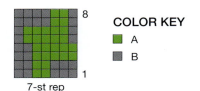

SUPER COZY
Because this scarf is knitted in the round, it creates a double-layer of fabric when worn for an extra warm scarf.

Pocket Scarf

DESIGNED BY Matthew Schrank

This fun garter-stitch scarf is as simple as can be: Knit one long rectangle, then turn up the ends and sew the sides together to form the pockets.

MEASUREMENTS
Width 5"/12.5cm
Length (with pockets folded) 40"/101.5cm

MATERIALS
- 3½oz/100g and 210yd/191m skein of any cotton/wool blend (3) 1 skein each in Pink (A) and Blue (B)
- One pair size 7 (4.5mm) needles, or size to obtain gauge

GAUGE
19 sts and 30 rows to 4"/10cm over garter st using size 7 (4.5mm) needles. *TAKE TIME TO CHECK YOUR GAUGE.*

SCARF
With A, cast on 24 sts. Work in garter st (k every row) for 48"/122cm. Bind off loosely.

Bows (make 2)
With B, cast on 13 sts. Work in garter st for 4"/10cm. Bind off.

CENTER BAND
With B, cast on 4 sts. Work in garter st for 2½"/6.5cm. Bind off.
Sew cast-on and bound-off edge tog to form a ring. Weave bow through center of ring.

Finishing
Weave in ends.

PICK A SEAM
Some patterns specify a method of seaming, often for a desired effect. If not specified, use your preferred method. For this project, mattress stitch or overcast stitch would do nicely.

Bow Scarf

DESIGNED BY Sandi Prosser

A simple texture is the perfect accent for an oversized bow in this fun accessory that's perfect for any kid who enjoys a bit of whimsy.

MEASUREMENTS
Width 4"/10cm
Length 42"/106.5cm

MATERIALS
- 1¾oz/50g and 85yd/78m skeins in any cotton (4) 3 skeins in Pink
- One pair size 7 (4.5mm) needles, *or size to obtain gauge*
- Stitch markers
- One snap fastener
- Sewing needle and thread

GAUGE
20 sts and 30 rows to 4"/10cm over moss st using size 7 (4.5mm) needles. *TAKE TIME TO CHECK YOUR GAUGE.*

MOSS STITCH
(multiple of 4 sts)
Row 1 (RS) K3, *p2, k2; rep from* to last st, k1.
Rows 2 and 3 K1, *p2, k2; rep from * to last 3 sts, p2, k1.
Row 4 K3, *p2, k2; rep from* to last st, k1.
Rep rows 1–4 for moss st.

SCARF
Cast on 20 sts. Work in moss st for 42"/106.5cm, end with a WS row. Bind off in pat.

Bow
Cast on 20 sts. Work in moss st for 16"/40.5cm, end with a WS row. Bind off in pat.

TIE
Cast on 8 sts. Work in moss st for 4½"/11.5cm, end with a WS row. Bind off in pat.

Finishing
Weave in ends.
Lay scarf flat. Place markers approx 11"/28cm from each end at center of scarf width.
Sew cast-on and bound-off sts of bow tog. Fold bow in half, placing seam at center back. Place bow over one marker on scarf. Using a small length of yarn, tie yarn around center of bow and scarf, gathering tightly.
Wrap tie around center of bow and scarf, and then sew bound-off and cast-on edges of tie tog. Secure tie with several straight sts to bow and scarf.
Sew one side of snap fastener to back of tie and other side of snap fastener to scarf to hold the bow in place.

PLAYING WITH SCALE
For simple shapes knit in a simple stitch pattern, like the pieces of this bow, you could easily add or remove repeats to adjust the completed size. If scaling larger, just make sure you'll have enough yarn!

Textured Cowl

DESIGNED BY Audrey Drysdale

A cozy cowl is worked in the round with alternating bands of reverse stockinette and moss stitch. Short-row shaping at the back helps it sit better when pulled up and worn as a snood.

MEASUREMENTS
Width 4½"/11.5cm
Length 20"/51cm

MEASUREMENTS
Circumference 25"/63.5cm
Length (center back) 21"/165cm

MATERIALS
- 3½oz/100g and 194yd/177m skein of any wool (4) 2 skeins in Gray
- One size 7 (4.5mm) circular needle, 24"/60cm long, *or size to obtain gauge*
- Stitch marker

GAUGE
20 sts and 26 rnds to 4"/10cm over St st using size 7 (4.5mm) needle.
TAKE TIME TO CHECK YOUR GAUGE.

COWL
Cast on 124 sts. Join, taking care not to twist sts, and pm for beg of rnd.
Rnds 1–7 Purl.
Rnd 8 Knit.
Rnds 9 and 10 *K1, p1; rep from * around.
Rnds 11 and 12 *P1, k1; rep from * around.
Rnds 13–18 Rep rnds 9–12 once, then rnds 9 and 10 once more.
Rnd 19 Knit.
Rep rounds 1–19 for pat 4 times more.

Shape Back
****Next 3 rnds** Purl.
Work in short-rows (see page 174) as foll:
Short-row 1 (RS) P45, w&t.
Short-row 2 (WS) K45, sm, k45, w&t.
Short-row 3 P45, sm, p35, w&t.
Short-row 4 K35, sm, k35, w&t.
Short-row 5 P35, sm, p25, w&t.
Short-row 6 K25, sm, k25, w&t.

Cont in rnds as foll:
Next rnd (RS) P25, sm, p to end of rnd, picking up wraps.
Next 3 rnds Purl.++
Next rnd Knit.
Next 2 rnd *K1, p1; rep from * around.
Next 2 rnds *P1, k1; rep from * around.
Next 6 rnds Rep last 4 rnds once more, then rep first 2 rnds once.
Next rnd Knit.**

Rep from ** to ** once more, then from ** to ++ once.
Bind off purlwise.

Finishing
Weave in ends. Block to measurements.

SKIP IT
If you don't intend to ever wear this cowl as a snood (or just want a simpler knit), work rounds 1–19 a total of 7 times and skip the short-row shaping.

Opposites Dolman Pullover

DESIGNED BY Deborah Newton

Clever color blocking and cool dolman sleeves—increased on either side of the back and front pieces—give this casual sweater real cachet.

SIZES
Small (Medium, Large, 1X, 2X). Shown in size Medium.

MEASUREMENTS
Bust 45½ (49, 53, 57, 60½)"/115.5 (124.5, 134.5, 144.5, 153.5)cm
Length 19 (19½, 19½, 20, 20)"/48 (49.5, 49.5, 51, 51)cm
Upper arm 19 (20, 20, 21, 21)"/48 (51, 51, 53.5, 53.5)cm

MATERIALS
- 1¾oz/50g and 131yd/120m skein of any alpaca/wool/polyamide blend
- 4 (4, 5, 5, 6) skeins each in Pink (A) and Gray (B)
- One each size 8 and 9 (5 and 5.5mm) circular needle, each 32"/80cm long, *or size to obtain gauge*
- Stitch markers
- Stitch holders

GAUGE
17 sts and 22 rows to 4"/10cm over St st using larger needles.
TAKE TIME TO CHECK YOUR GAUGE.

SWEATER
Back
With smaller needle and A, cast on 78 (86, 94, 102, 110) sts.
Row 1 (WS) P2, *k2, p2; rep from * to end.
Row 2 (RS) K2, *p2, k2; rep from * to end.
Rep last 2 rows for k2, p2 rib for 2½"/6.5cm, end with a WS row and dec 7 sts evenly on last row—71 (79, 87, 95, 103) sts. Cut A.

BODY
Change to larger needle and join B.
Row 1 (RS) Knit.
Row 2 Purl.
Inc row 3 K3, M1, k to last 3 sts, M1, k3—2 sts inc'd.
Row 4 Purl.
Row 5 Rep row 3—2 sts inc'd.
Row 6 Purl.
Rep last 6 rows 5 times more, then rep rows 1–4 once more—97 (105, 113, 121, 129) sts.

SHAPE DOLMAN SLEEVE
Cont in St st, cast on 3 sts at beg of next 28 rows—181 (189, 197, 205, 213) sts.
Work even in St st until piece measures 3½ (4, 4, 4½, 4½)"/9 (10, 10, 11.5, 11.5)cm from last cast-on row, end with a WS row.

SHAPE NECK
Mark center 39 sts.
Next row (RS) K to center 39 sts, join 2nd ball of B and bind off center 39 sts, k to end.
Cont in St st, working both sides as foll:
Next dec row (WS) For first shoulder, p all sts; for 2nd shoulder, bind off 2 sts, p to end.
Next dec row (RS) For first shoulder, k all sts; for 2nd shoulder, bind off 2 sts, k to end.
Rep last 2 rows twice more.
Place rem 65 (69, 73, 77, 81) sts each side on st holders.

Front
With smaller needle and B, cast on 78 (86, 94, 102, 110) sts.
Row 1 (WS) P2, *k2, p2; rep from * to end.
Row 2 (RS) K2, *p2, k2; rep from * to end.
Rep last 2 rows for k2, p2 rib for 2"/5cm, end with a WS row and dec 7 sts evenly on last row—71 (79, 87, 95, 103) sts. Cut B.

TAKE IT EASY
While this pattern may look intimidating, the stitch patterns and techniques are all simple. Take things one step at a time, and be patient with yourself. You can do it!

BODY

Change to larger needle and join A.
With A, complete same as for back.

Finishing

Weave in ends. Block pieces lightly to measurements.
Leaving ribbing unseamed for side vent, sew side seams using mattress st over St st (see page 182), beg above ribbing and seaming to sleeve cuff.
Place shoulder sts on needles and join shoulders using 3-needle bind-off (see page 173).

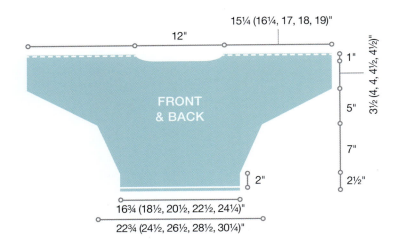

SLEEVE TRIM

With smaller needle, RS facing and A, pick up and k 30 (30, 30, 34, 34) sts evenly along back (B) edge of sleeve.
Work in k2, p2 rib same as for back for 1½"/4cm. Bind off.
With smaller needle, RS facing and B, pick up and k 30 (30, 30, 34, 34) sts evenly along front (A) edge of sleeve.
Work in k2, p2 rib same as for back for 1½"/4cm. Bind off.
Seam only first couple of sts of front and back sleeve trims using mattress st over St st, leaving the rest unseamed.

BACK NECKLINE TRIM

With smaller needle, RS facing and A, pick up and k 66 sts evenly along back (B) edge.
Work in k2, p2 rib same as for back for 6 rows.
Short-rows 1 and 2 Work to last 11 sts, w&t (see page 174), work to last 11 sts, w&t.
Short-rows 3 and 4 Work to 10 sts before last wrapped st, w&t, work to 10 sts before last wrapped st, w&t.
Short-rows 5 and 6 Work ribbing as established over all sts, closing wraps as you come to them.
Short-rows 7 and 8 Work to 6 sts before last wrapped st, w&t, work to 6 sts before last wrapped st, w&t.
Short-rows 9 and 10 Work ribbing as established over all sts, closing wraps as you come to them.

Cont in rib until trim measures 2½"/6.5cm, measured at side edges, end with a WS row.
Bind off in rib.

FRONT NECKLINE TRIM

With smaller needle, RS facing and B, pick up and k 66 sts evenly along front (A) edge.
Work in k2, p2 rib until trim measures 2½"/6.5cm, end with a WS row. Bind off in rib.

Sew side seams of front and back neckline trim using mattress st.

Pebble Yoke Pullover

DESIGNED BY Yelena M. Dasher

A slip-stitch texture adorns the yoke, cuffs, and hem of this seamless pullover. The clever top-down construction offers a speedy knit and flattering shaped silhouette.

PEBBLE STITCH IN ROWS
(odd number of sts)
Row 1 (RS) Knit.
Row 2 K1, *sl 1 wyib, k1; rep from * to end.
Row 3 Knit.
Row 4 K2, *sl 1 wyib, k1; rep from * to last st, k1.
Rep rows 1–4 for pebble stitch in rows.

PEBBLE STITCH IN ROUNDS
(an even number of sts)
Rnd 1 Knit.
Rnd 2 *P1, sl 1 wyif; rep from * around.
Rnd 3 Knit.
Rnd 4 *Sl 1 wyif, p1; rep from * around.
Rep rnds 1–4 for pebble st in rnds.

PULLOVER
Back
RIGHT BACK SHOULDER
Cast on 23 (25, 27, 29, 31) sts. Work in pebble st in rows for 4 rows. Place sts on a st holder.

LEFT BACK SHOULDER
Work same as for right back shoulder.

JOIN SHOULDERS
Joining row (RS) K the 23 (25, 27, 29, 31) sts of left back shoulder, turn to WS and cast on 31 sts for neck, turn work to RS and k the 23 (25, 27, 29, 31) sts of right

back shoulder—77 (81, 85, 89, 93) sts. Working across all back sts, work even until piece measures 6 (6½, 7, 7½, 8)"/15 (16.5, 18, 19, 20.5)cm. place sts on scrap yarn.

Front
LEFT FRONT SHOULDER
With RS facing, pick up and k 23 (25, 27, 29, 31) sts along cast-on edge of left back shoulder.
Beg with row 2 on WS, work pebble st in rows for 10 rows. Place sts on a st holder.

SIZES
Small (Medium, Large, X-Large, XX-Large). Shown in size Medium.

MEASUREMENTS
Bust 36 (38, 40, 42, 44)"/91.5 (96.5, 101.5, 106.5, 111.5)cm
Length 23 (23½, 24, 24½, 25)"/58.5 (59.5, 61, 62, 63.5)cm
Upper arm 12½ (13½, 14½, 15½, 16½)"/31.5 (34, 37, 39.5, 42)cm

MATERIALS
- 3½oz/100g and 200yd/199m skein of any wool/silk blend (4)
  5 (5, 6, 6, 7) skeins in Purple
- One pair size 8 (5mm) needles, *or size to obtain gauge*
- One size 8 (5mm) circular needle, 29"/74cm long
- One set (5) size 8 (5mm) double-pointed needles (dpn)
- Stitch markers
- Stitch holder
- Scrap yarn

GAUGE
17 sts and 25 rows/rnds to 4"/10cm over St st using size 8 (5mm) needles.
TAKE TIME TO CHECK YOUR GAUGE.

NOTE
Pullover begins at shoulder edge with back and front worked separately to the armhole. Then, pieces are joined to work in rounds for the body. The sleeves are picked up along the armhole edges and worked to the cuffs.

Right shoulder

With RS facing, pick up and k 23 (25, 27, 29, 31) sts from cast-on edge of right back shoulder. Beg with row 2 on WS, work pebble st in rows for 10 rows. Do not place sts on a st holder.

JOIN SHOULDERS

Change to circular needle.
Joining row (RS) K the 23 (25, 27, 29, 31) sts of right front shoulder, turn to WS and cast on 31 sts for neck, turn work to RS and k the 23 (25, 27, 29, 31) sts of left front shoulder—77 (81, 85, 89, 93) sts. Work even until piece measures same as back with same number of rows from shoulder.

Body

Rnd 1 K the back sts then k the front sts—154 (162, 170, 178, 186) sts.
Join to work in rnds and pm to mark beg of rnd.
Cont in St st (k every rnd), for 3"/7.5cm.
Set-up rnd K26 (27, 28, 30, 31), pm, k26 (27, 28, 29, 31), pm, k51 (54, 57, 60, 62), pm, k26 (27, 28, 29, 31), pm, k25 (27, 29, 30, 31).
Dec rnd *K to 2 sts before marker, ssk, sm, k to next marker, sm, k2tog; rep from * once more, k to end—4 sts dec'd.
Cont in St st, rep dec rnd every 10th row 3 times more—138 (146, 154, 162, 170) sts.
Work even until body measures 9"/23cm from underarm.
Inc rnd *K to 1 st before marker, kfb, sm, k to next marker, sm, kfb; rep from * once more, k to end—4 sts inc'd.
Rep inc rnd every 6th rnd 3 times more—154 (162, 170, 178, 186) sts.
Work even until body measures 15½"/39.5cm.
Work pebble st in rnds for 16 rnds.
Bind off.

Sleeves

With dpn, pick up and k 54 (58, 62, 66, 70) sts evenly around armhole edge, dividing sts over 4 dpn with 13 (14, 15, 16, 17) sts on needles 1 and 3 and 14 (15, 16, 17, 18) sts on needles 2 and 4.
Join and work St st in rnds (k every rnd) for 2¼"/6cm.
Dec rnd K1, k2tog, k to last 3 sts, ssk, k1—2 sts dec'd.
Cont in St st, rep dec rnd every 7th rnd 12 (12, 12, 13, 13) times more—28 (32, 36, 38, 42) sts.
Work even until sleeve measures 18"/45.5cm.
Work pebble st in rnds for 16 rnds. Bind off.
Rep for 2nd sleeve at rem armhole edge.

Finishing

Weave in ends. Block to measurements.

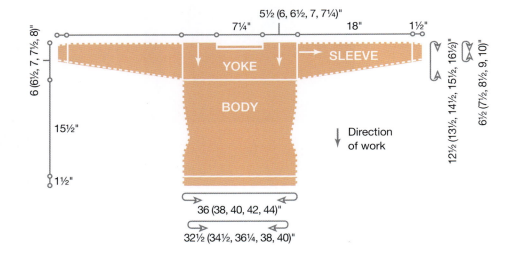

Blaze Pullover

DESIGNED BY Audrey Drysdale

A textural pattern—the loop lying between two stitches is picked up and passed over the next two knit stitches—gives this sweater extra oomph.

SIZES
Small (Medium, Large, X-Large, XX-Large, 1X). Shown in size Medium.

MEASUREMENTS
Bust 38 (41, 44, 47, 49, 52)"/96.5 (104, 111.5, 119, 124.5, 132)cm
Length 24 (24½, 24½, 25, 25½, 26)"/61 (62, 62, 63.5, 65, 66)cm
Upper arm 16½ (17¼, 17¼, 18, 18¾, 19½)"/42 (44, 44, 45.5, 47.5, 49.5)cm

MATERIALS
- 7oz/200g and 437yd/400m skein of any baby alpaca
- 4 (4, 5, 5, 5, 5) balls in Yellow to Red Ombré
- One pair size 8 (5mm) needles, *or size to obtain gauge*
- Stitch holders
- Pins

GAUGE
23 sts and 26 rows to 4"/10cm over pat st using size 8 (5mm) needles.
TAKE TIME TO CHECK YOUR GAUGE.

NOTE
If you prefer a gradient similar to the one seen in the photos, use a different skein of yarn for each separate piece starting at the same point in the color sequence. Monitor the color changes as you work, removing sections of a color, if needed, to maintain the same rate of color change across all pieces.

PATTERN STITCH
(multiple of 4 sts plus 2)
Row 1 (RS) K1, *insert RH needle from back to front under horizontal strand between st just knit and next st on LH needle and leave this strand on RH needle, k next 2 sts, then pass picked-up strand over the 2 sts just knit, k2; rep from * to last st, k1.
Row 2 Purl.
Row 3 K3; rep from * in row 1 to last st 3 sts; insert RH needle from back to front under horizontal strand between st just knit and next st on LH needle and leave this strand on RH needle, k next 2 sts, then pass picked-up strand over the 2 sts just knit, k1.
Row 4 Purl.
Rep rows 1–4 for pat st.

PULLOVER
Back
Cast on 102 (110, 118, 126, 134, 142) sts.
Row 1 (RS) K2, *p2, k2; rep from * to end.
Row 2 P2, *k2, p2; rep from * to end.
Rep rows 1 and 2 once, then rep row 1 once more.
Next row (WS) Purl, inc'ing 8 sts evenly spaced—110 (118, 126, 134, 142, 150) sts.
Work even in pat st until piece measures 15½"/39.5cm from beg.

SHAPE ARMHOLE
Cont in pat, bind off 5 (5, 5, 6, 7, 7) sts at beg of next 2 rows.
Dec 1 st each side of next row then every other row 4 (5, 6, 6, 7, 8) times more—90 (96, 102, 108, 112, 118) sts.
Work even in pat until armhole measures 6½ (7, 7, 7½, 8, 8½)"/16.5 (18, 18, 19, 20.5, 21.5)cm.

SHAPE NECK
Next row (RS) Work 23 (25, 28, 31, 33, 36) sts, turn and place center 44 (46, 46, 46, 46, 46) sts on a st holder.

SHAPE RIGHT NECK
Cont in pat over right shoulder sts only, dec 1 st at neck edge on next 3 rows—20 (22, 25, 28, 30, 33) sts.
Work even in pat for 4 rows over these shoulder sts.

SHAPE RIGHT SHOULDER
Cont in pat, bind off 10 (11, 12, 14, 15, 16)

READY, SET, SLEEVE

Setting in (fitting) a sleeve cap (the curved top portion) into a shaped armhole takes patience. First, pin everything in place, then seam. If the seam or fabric looks lumpy or puckered, undo the seam and try again.

sts at shoulder edge (beg of RS row), then bind off 10 (11, 13, 14, 15, 17) sts at shoulder edge.

SHAPE LEFT NECK AND SHOULDER
With RS facing, rejoin yarn to rem 23 (25, 28, 31, 33, 36) sts.
Cont in pat, dec 1 st at neck edge on next 3 rows—20 (22, 25, 28, 30, 33) sts. Work even for 4 rows over these shoulder sts.

SHAPE LEFT SHOULDER
Cont in pat, bind off 10 (11, 12, 14, 15, 16) sts at shoulder edge (beg of WS row), then bind off 10 (11, 13, 14, 15, 17) sts at shoulder edge.

Front
Work same as for back, including armhole shaping, until armhole measures 4½ (5, 5, 5½, 6, 6½)"/11.5 (12.5, 12.5, 14, 15, 16.5)cm, end with a WS row.

SHAPE NECK
Next row (RS) Work 28 (30, 33, 36, 38, 41) sts, turn and place center 34 (36, 36, 36, 36, 36) sts on a st holder.

SHAPE LEFT NECK
Cont in pat over left shoulder sts only, dec 1 st at neck edge on next 3 rows, then bind off 1 st at neck edge on next 5 RS rows—20 (22, 25, 28, 30, 33) sts rem. Work even until armhole measures 7½ (8, 8, 8½, 9, 9½)"/19 (20.5, 20.5, 21.5, 23, 24)cm.

SHAPE LEFT SHOULDER
Cont in pat, bind off 10 (11, 12, 14, 15, 16) sts from shoulder edge (beg of WS row), then 10 (11, 13, 14, 15, 17) sts at shoulder edge.

SHAPE RIGHT NECK
Rejoin yarn to rem 28 (30, 33, 36, 38, 41) sts to work next row from RS. Dec 1 st at neck edge on next 3 rows, then dec 1 st at neck edge on next 5 RS rows—20 (22, 25, 28, 30, 33) sts.
Work even until armhole measures 7½ (8, 8, 8½, 9, 9½)"/19 (20.5, 20.5, 21.5, 23, 24) cm.

SHAPE RIGHT SHOULDER
Cont in pat, bind off 10 (11, 12, 14, 15, 16) sts from shoulder edge (beg of RS row), then 10 (11, 13, 14, 15, 17) sts at shoulder edge.

Sleeves
Cast on 50 (54, 54, 58, 58, 62) sts.
Work k2, p2 rib same as for back for 5 rows.
Next row (WS) Purl, inc'ing 8 sts evenly spaced—58 (62, 62, 66, 66, 70) sts.
Work even in pat st for 6 rows.
Cont in pat, inc 1 st each side of next row then every 4th row 0 (3, 3, 3, 8, 8) times more, then every 6th row 17 (15, 15, 15, 12, 12) times—94 (100, 100, 104, 108, 112) sts.
Work even until piece measures 18½"/47cm from beg.

SHAPE CAP
Cont in pat, bind off 5 (5, 5, 6, 7, 7) sts at beg of next 2 rows.
Dec 1 st each side of next row then every other row 4 (5, 6, 6, 7, 8) times more—74 (78, 76, 78, 78, 80) sts. Bind off.

Finishing
Weave in ends. Lay a wet cloth on pieces and block to measurements.
Sew left shoulder seam.

NECKBAND
With RS facing, pick up and k 9 sts from shaped back neck edge; then k44 (46, 46, 46, 46, 46) sts from back neck holder while dec'ing 6 sts evenly across these sts; then pick up and k 9 sts from shaped back neck edge; then pick up and k 28 sts from shaped front neck edge; then k34 (36, 36, 36, 36, 36) sts from front neck holder while dec'ing 4 sts evenly

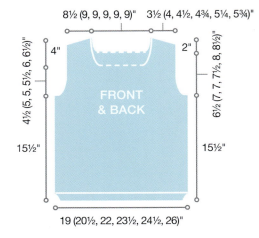

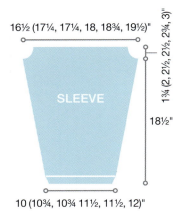

spaced across these sts; and then pick up and k 28 sts from shaped front neck edge—142 (146, 146, 146, 146, 146) sts. Work in rows of k2, p2 rib same as for back for 7 rows. Bind off in rib.

Sew other shoulder and neckband seams.

Pin sleeve caps into armholes with top center of sleeve caps at shoulder seams and edges of sleeve caps at first underarm bind-offs of body. Seam sleeves in place.

Sew side and sleeve seams. Weave in rem ends. ∎

Chevron Pullover

DESIGNED BY Yelena M. Dasher

Knit and purl stitches create the textured chevron pattern in this top-down sweater.

PULLOVER
Back
RIGHT BACK SHOULDER
With larger needles, cast on 33 (37, 41, 41) sts. Knit 1 row on WS.

BEGIN CHART PATTERN
Row 1 (RS) Working row 1 of chart, beg with st 1 (5, 1, 1), work to rep line, then work 8-st rep 3 (3, 4, 4) times more, end with st 9.
Rows 2–7 Work chevron pat foll chart as established.
At end of row 7 (RS), turn work and cast on 23 (23, 23, 31) sts for neck. Lay piece aside.

LEFT BACK SHOULDER
With larger needles, cast on 33 (37, 41, 41) sts. Knit 1 row on WS.
Row 1 (RS) Working row 1 of chart, beg with st 1 and work 8-st rep for 4 (4, 5, 5) reps, then work sts 1–4 for 0 (1, 0, 0) time(s) more, end with st 9 (5, 9, 9).
Rows 2–7 Work chevron pat foll chart as established.

JOIN SHOULDERS
Joining row (WS) Work as established on 33 (37, 41, 41) sts of left back shoulder, cont in pat across 23 (23, 23, 31) cast-on sts for neck, work rem sts in established pat—89 (97, 105, 113) sts.
Cont in chevron pat until armhole measures 6¾ (7½, 8½, 8¾)"/17 (19, 21.5, 22)cm. Place sts on scrap yarn.

Front
RIGHT FRONT SHOULDER
With larger needle and from RS, pick up and k 33 (37, 41, 41) sts from cast-on edge of right back shoulder.
Row 2 (WS) Beg with st 9 of chart row 2, work 8-st rep for 4 (4, 5, 5) reps, end with st 1 (5, 1, 1).
Rows 3–8 Work even foll chart.
Inc row 9 (RS) Work pat st to last st, M1 (k or p to inc into pat), k1.
Rep inc row (for neck) every RS row 3 times more—37 (41, 45, 45) sts.
Work row 16 of chart. Place sts on scrap yarn.

LEFT FRONT SHOULDER
With larger needles and from RS, pick up and k 33 (37, 41, 41) sts from cast-on edge of left back shoulder.
Row 2 (WS) Beg with st 1 of chart row 2, work 8-st rep for 4 (4, 5, 5) reps, then work sts 1–4 for 0 (1, 0, 0) times more, end with st 9 (5, 9, 9).
Rows 3–8 Work even foll chart.
Inc row 9 (RS) K1, M1 (k or p to inc into pat), work to end.
Rep inc row (for neck) every RS row 3 times more—37 (41, 45, 45) sts.
Work row 16 of chart.

JOIN SHOULDERS
Next row (RS) Work row 1 of chart over right shoulder sts, cast on 15 (15, 15, 23) sts for center front neck, work across left shoulder sts in pat—89 (97, 105, 113) sts.
Work even in pat until there are same number of rows as on back to armhole.

SIZES
Small (Medium, Large, X-Large). Shown in size Small.

MEASUREMENTS
Bust 35½ (39, 42, 45¼)"/90 (99, 106.5, 115)cm
Length 23½ (24¼, 25¼, 25½)"/59.5 (61.5, 64, 65)cm
Upper arm 13¼ (14¾, 16½, 18)"/33.5 (37.5, 42, 45.5)cm

MATERIALS
- 3½oz/100g and 191yd/175m skein of any superwash wool (4) 6 (7, 8, 9) skeins in Green
- One pair each sizes 6 and 8 (4 and 5mm) needles, *or size to obtain gauge*
- One each size 6 and 8 (4 and 5mm) circular needles, each 29"/74cm long
- One size 6 (4mm) circular needle, 16"/40cm long
- One set (5) each size 6 and 8 (4 and 5mm) double-pointed needles (dpn)
- Stitch markers
- Stitch holders
- Scrap yarn

GAUGE
20 sts and 28 rows/rnds to 4"/10cm over chart using larger needles.
TAKE TIME TO CHECK YOUR GAUGE.

NOTE
Pullover is worked by beginning with the shoulder edge, then back and front are worked separately to the armhole. Then, pieces are joined to work in rounds for the body and the sleeves are picked up along the armhole edges and worked to the cuffs.

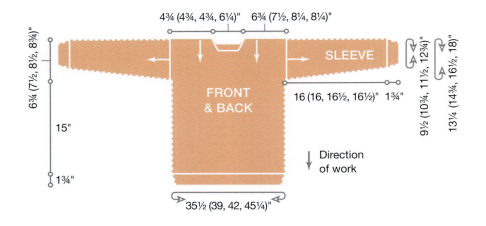
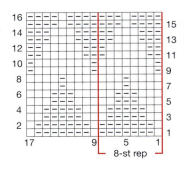

STITCH KEY
☐ k on RS, p on WS
⊟ p on RS, k on WS

Body
Note When working body in rounds, cont to work in pat as established on each piece, that is in two identical pieces matched at underarm edges (not a continuous pat). Work each row of chart from right to left.
Next rnd Work chart as established across back sts, then work chart as established across front sts, pm, and join to work in rnds—178 (194, 210, 226) sts. Work even until piece measures 15"/38cm from beg.
Change to smaller circular needle.
Next 12 rnds *K1, p1; rep from * around.
Bind off using larger needle.

Sleeves
With larger dpn, pick up and k 66 (74, 82, 90) sts evenly around armhole edge, dividing sts over 4 dpn with 16 (18, 20, 22) sts on needles 1 and 3 and 17 (19, 21, 23) sts on needles 2 and 4.
Join to work in rnds.
Rnd 1 K1 (selvage st), work 8-st rep for 7 (8, 9, 10) reps, work sts 9-17.
Work even over chart as established for 2"/5cm.
Dec rnd K1, dec 1 st (k2tog when first st is a k st or p2tog when first st is a p st), work pat to last 4 sts, dec 1 st (by SKP for a k st or p2tog for a p st), work 1 st, k1. Rep dec rnd every 8th rnd 8 (9, 11, 12) times more—48 (54, 58, 64) sts.
Work even until sleeve measures 16 (16, 16½, 16½)"/40.5 (40.5, 42, 42)cm from beg. Change to smaller dpn and work in k1, p1 rib for 12 rnds.
Bind off using larger needle.

Finishing
NECKBAND
With RS facing and shorter circular needle, pick up and k 70 (70, 70, 86) sts around neck edge. Join to work in rnds and pm for beg of rnd.
Work in k1, p1 rib for 12 rnds.
Bind off using larger needle.

Weave in ends. Lightly block to measurements on WS of piece.

INCREASING INTO PATTERN
When working the increases for the front neck, increase by making a purl or knit stitch as you would need to continue the pattern in that given row.

Snowfall Sweater

DESIGNED BY Sandi Rosner

Knit in the round from the top down, this pint-sized sweater is yoked with Scandinavian-style snowflakes. The rolled trims at the neckline and cuffs are folded under and stitched loosely to the wrong side.

SIZES
Sized for Child's 2 (4, 6, 8). Shown in size Child's 4.

MEASUREMENTS
Chest 24½ (26, 27, 29½)"/62 (66, 68.5, 75)cm
Length 13½ (14, 16, 18)"/34 (35.5, 40.5, 45.5)cm
Upper arm 8¾ (9, 10, 11)"/22 (23, 25.5, 28)cm

MATERIALS
- 1¾oz/50g and 136yd/124m skein of any wool (3)
  3 (4, 4, 5) skeins in Red (A)
  1 skein in White (B)
- One size 6 (4mm) circular needle, 16"/40cm long, *or size to obtain gauge*
- One each size 4 and 6 (3.5 and 4mm) circular needle, each 24"/60cm long
- One set (5) each size 4 and 6 (3.5 and 4mm) double-pointed needles (dpn)
- Stitch markers
- Scrap yarn

GAUGE
22 sts and 30 rnds to 4"/10cm over St st using larger needle.
TAKE TIME TO CHECK YOUR GAUGE.

NOTE
Pullover is knit in rounds from the top down. Short-rows are worked to shape the front neck.

SWEATER
Yoke
With smaller dpn and A, cast on 64 sts, dividing sts evenly over 4 dpn with 16 sts on each needle. Join, taking care not to twist sts, and pm for beg of rnd.
Purl 6 rnds. Knit 1 rnd.
Change to size 6 (4mm) 16"/40cm circular needle.
Inc rnd [K1, kfb] 32 times—96 sts.

SHORT-ROW SHAPING
Short-row 1 (RS) K26, w&t (see page 174).
Short-row 2 (WS) Sl 1, p52, w&t.
Short-row 3 Sl 1, k to wrapped st, close up wrap, k5, w&t.
Short-row 4 Sl 1, p to wrapped st, close up wrap, p5, w&t.
Short-rows 5 and 6 Rep short-rows 3 and 4.
Short-row 7 K to beg of rnd marker.
Next rnd Knit, closing up all wraps.
Knit 3 rnds.
Change to size 6 (4mm) 24"/60cm circular needle.
Inc rnd [K3, M1] 32 times—128 sts.

CHART
Join B.
Rnd 1 Work 16-st rep of chart 8 times around.
Work chart as established through rnd 15. Cut B.

Cont with A only.

Next rnd Knit.
Inc rnd [K3, M1] 42 times, k2—170 sts.
Knit 6 rnds.
Inc rnd [K5, M1] 34 times—204 sts.
Knit 2 (3, 6, 6) rnds.

SIZE 4 ONLY
Inc rnd K12, [M1, k20] 9 times, M1, k12—214 sts.

FOR SIZES 6 (8) ONLY
Inc rnd [K8, M1] 25 times, k4, M1—230 sts.
Knit 4 (6) rnds.

FOR SIZE 8 ONLY
Inc rnd [K9, M1] 24 times, k14—254 sts.
Knit 6 rnds.

FOR ALL SIZES
There are 204 (214, 230, 254) sts.

Divide for Body and Sleeves
Next rnd K30 (32, 33, 37) for half of back; place next 41 (42, 48, 53) sts on scrap yarn for sleeve; turn to WS and cast on 7 sts for underarm; turn to RS and k61 (65, 67, 74) for front; place next 41 (42, 48, 53) sts on scrap yarn for sleeve; turn to WS and cast on 7 sts for underarm; turn to RS and k31 (33, 34, 37) sts for half of back—136 (144, 148, 162) sts total for body.

Body
Work in St st (k every rnd) until piece measures 6½ (7½, 7½, 8½)"/16.5 (19, 19,

TACK IN PLACE
To tack something in place means to sew it down using loose stitches of your choice. Just make sure the stitches do not show through on the right side of your work.

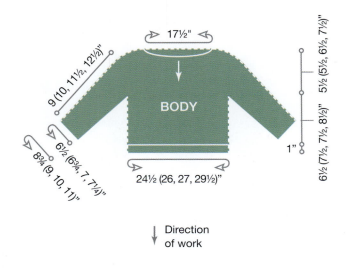
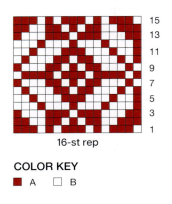

COLOR KEY
■ A □ B

21.5)cm from underarm cast-on sts. Change to size 4 (3.5mm) circular needle.
Next rnd Work in k2, p2 rib dec'ing 0 (0, 0, 2) sts evenly spaced—136 (144, 148, 160) sts.
Cont in k2, p2 rib until rib measures 1"/2.5cm. Bind off in rib.

Sleeves
With RS facing and larger dpn and beg at center of underarm, pick up and k 3 sts, k41 (42, 48, 53) sts on scrap yarn for sleeve, and then pick up and k 4 sts in rem underarm sts—48 (49, 55, 60) sts. Divide sts over 3 dpn. Knit 9 rnds.
Dec rnd K1, ssk, k to last 3 sts, k2tog, k1—2 sts dec'd.
Cont in St st, rep dec rnd every 10th (10th, 8th, 8th) rnd 5 (5, 7, 9) times more—36 (37, 39, 40) sts.
Work even until sleeve measures 9 (10, 11½, 12½)"/23 (25.5, 29, 32)cm.
Change to smaller dpn.
Next rnd Knit, dec'ing 6 (3, 3, 2) sts evenly spaced—30 (34, 36, 38) sts.
Purl 6 rnds. Bind off loosely.
Work second sleeve in same way.

Finishing
Turn rolled cuffs on sleeve to WS and tack in place.
Turn rolled neckband to WS and tack in place.
Weave in ends. Block to measurements.

Honey Pullover

DESIGNED BY Bonnie Franz

A unique construction has front and back worked from the top down separately from the same provisional cast-on. A simple stripe pattern and classic ribbing complete the look.

SIZES
X-Small (Small, Medium, Large, X-Large, XX-Large). Shown in size Small.

MEASUREMENTS
Bust 34 (36, 38¼, 42½, 45½, 48½)"/86 (91.5, 97, 108, 115.5, 123)cm
Length 22¼ (22¾, 23, 24¼, 25, 25½)"/56.5 (58, 58.5, 60, 63.5, 65)cm
Upper arm 15½ (16½, 17½, 19½, 20½, 21½)"/39.5 (42, 44.5, 49.5, 52, 54.5)cm

MATERIALS
- 1¾oz/50g and 122yd/112m skeins of any superwash wool ( )
  6 (6, 7, 8, 8, 9) skeins in Yellow (A)
  3 (3, 4, 4, 5, 5) skeins in White (B)
- One each size 5 and 7 (3.75 and 4.5mm) circular needle, each 36"/90cm long, *or size to obtain gauge*
- One pair each size 5 and 7 (3.75 and 4.5mm) needles
- Removable stitch markers
- Stitch holders
- Scrap yarn

GAUGE
19 sts and 24 rows/rnds to 4"/10cm over St st using larger needles.
TAKE TIME TO CHECK YOUR GAUGE.

NOTE
Pullover is worked from the shoulder edge down to the lower hem edge with stitches for the sleeves picked up along the armhole openings.

STRIPE PATTERN
Working St st in either rows (knit 1 row, purl 1 row) or rnds (knit every rnd), work stripes as foll:
*2 rows (rnds) in A; 2 rows (rnds) in B; 2 rows (rnds) A.
Rep these 6 rows (rnds) for stripe pat.

PULLOVER
Back
Beg at neck/shoulder edge with larger needles and A, using provisional cast-on (see page 169), cast on 68 (73, 78, 88, 93, 98) sts.
Work in 6-row stripe pat for 7¾ (8¼, 8½, 10, 10½, 11)"/19.5 (21, 21.5, 25.5, 26.5, 28)cm (top of armhole).
Place sts on scrap yarn.

Front
Carefully remove provisional cast-on and from RS, placing 20 (22, 24, 28, 30, 32) sts to larger needle for right shoulder, center 28 (29, 30, 32, 33, 34) sts on a st holder for back neck, and next 20 (22, 24, 28, 30, 32) sts to needle for left shoulder. Join separate small balls of A to each shoulder edge. Working each side

separately, beg with first row of stripe pat, shape neck as foll:
Work even in 6-row stripe pat on sts each side for 14 rows. Then, inc 1 st at each inside neck edge on next 8 rows—28 (30, 32, 36, 38, 40) sts each side.
On next row, cast on 12 (13, 14, 16, 17, 18) sts at center (neck) edge to join 2 shoulders—68 (73, 78, 88, 93, 98) sts. Work even in pat until there are same number of rows as on back to top of armhole. Place sts on scrap yarn.

Sleeves

With larger needles and A, with RS facing, pick up and k 76 (81, 85, 95, 100, 105) sts evenly along one armhole edge.
Working 6-row stripe pat (beg with 4 rows A), work even for 9 (9, 9, 9, 11, 13) rows. Pm on each side of last row.
Cont in stripe pat, dec'ing 1 st each side on next row, then every 6th (6th, 6th, 4th, 4th, 4th) row 10 (6, 6, 22, 20, 18) times more, then every 4th (4th, 4th, 2nd, 2nd, 2nd) row 8 (14, 14, 2, 5, 8) times—38 (39, 43, 45, 48, 51) sts.
Work even until sleeve measures 18"/45.5cm from beg.
Cut B. Change to smaller needles and with A, work in k1, p1 rib for 1¾"/4.5cm. Bind off in rib.
Work other sleeve in same way.

Body

With larger circular needle, rejoin yarn with RS facing, work *68 (73, 78, 88, 93, 98) sts of back, pick up and k 13 (13, 13, 15, 17) sts along straight edge of sleeve to marker, then pick up and k same number of sts on other edge of sleeve from marker to body; rep from * across front sts and rem sleeve—162 (172, 182, 202, 216, 230) sts. Join and pm for beg of rnd.
Cont in St st and 6-rnd stripe pat until body measures 12"/30.5cm from underarm. Cut B. Change to smaller circular needle.
With A, work in k1, p1 rib for 2½"/6.5cm. Bind off in rib.

Finishing

Sew sleeve seams.

NECKBAND

With smaller circular needle and A, with RS facing, pick up and k 19 sts evenly along shaped front neck edge, pick up and k 12 (13, 14, 16, 17, 18) sts evenly from front neck cast-on, pick up and k 19 sts evenly along other front shaped neck edge, and k 28 (29, 30, 32, 33, 34) sts from back neck holder—78 (80, 82, 86, 88, 90) sts. Join and pm for beg of rnd.
Work in rnds of k1, p1 rib for 1¼"/3cm. Bind off in rib.

Weave in ends. Block to measurements.

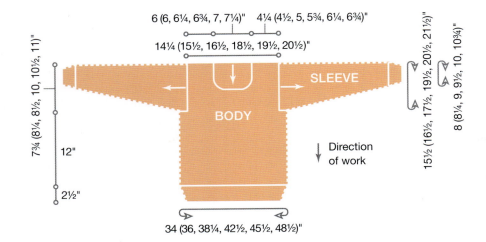

PICK YOUR FAVORITE
Some patterns list specific increases or decreases to use, but others give you a bit more freedom. This pattern states to "inc 1" or "dec 1" and allows you to use your favorite methods.

Toasty Tot Sweater

DESIGNED BY Renée Lorion

Earn your stripes by knitting some for a special little one in your life. A raglan sweater, knit in pieces from the bottom up, boasts a staggered stripe pattern. See pages 22 and 23 for a companion hat.

SIZES
6 months (12 months, 18 months, 24 months). Shown in 12 months.

MEASUREMENTS
Chest 19 (21, 22, 23)"/48 (53.5, 56, 58.5)cm
Length 10 (10½, 11¼, 11¾)"/25.5 (26.5, 28.5, 30)cm
Upper arm 8 (8½, 9, 9½)"/20.5 (21.5, 23, 24)cm

MATERIALS
- 3½oz/100g and 217yd/200m skein of any acrylic/wool/nylon blend (4) 1 skein each in Blue (A) and Tan (B)
- One pair size 7 (4.5mm) needles, or size to obtain gauge
- One size 7 (4.5mm) circular needle, 12"/30cm long

GAUGE
18 sts and 24 rnds to 4"/10cm over St st using size 7 (4.5mm) needles.
TAKE TIME TO CHECK YOUR GAUGE.

STRIPE PATTERN
Work 2 rows in B; 4 rows in A; 4 rows in B; 2 rows in A; 2 rows in B; 4 rows in A; 2 rows in B; cont to end with A only.

SWEATER
Back
With A, cast on 43 (47, 49, 51) sts.
Work in k1, p1 rib for 4 rows.
Work in St st (k on RS, p on WS) until piece measures 5¼ (5¾, 5¾, 6¼)"/13.5 (14.5, 14.5, 16)cm from beg, end with a WS row.
With CC, work 2 rows.

BEG STRIPE PAT AND SHAPE RAGLAN ARMHOLE
Working in stripe pat, bind off 2 sts at beg of next 2 rows—39 (43, 45, 47) sts.
Work 0 (0, 2, 2) rows even.
Dec row (RS) K1, SKP, k to last 3 sts, k2tog, k1—2 sts dec'd.
Next row Purl.
Rep last 2 rows 8 (8, 9, 9) times more—21 (25, 25, 27) sts.
Dec row (RS) K1, SKP, k4, bind off center 7 (11, 11, 13) sts, k4, k2tog, k1.
Working both sides at once, bind off 3 sts at each neck edge once, bind off rem 3 sts each side.
Next dec row (WS) For first shoulder, work all sts; for 2nd shoulder, bind off 3 sts, work to end.
Next dec row (RS) For first shoulder, work all sts; for 2nd shoulder, bind off 3 sts, work to end.
Bind off rem sts.

Front
Work same as for back.

Sleeves
With A, cast on 26 (28, 31, 33) sts.
Work in k1, p1 rib for 4 rows.
Work 3 rows in St st.
Inc row K1, kfb, k to last 2 sts, kfb, k1—2 sts inc'd.
Cont in St st, rep inc row every 4th (6th, 6th, 6th) row 1 (2, 1, 0) times, then every 6th (8th, 8th, 8th) row 3 (2, 3, 4) times—36 (38, 41, 43) sts.
Work even until piece measures 5¾ (6¾, 7¼, 7¾)"/14.5 (17, 18.5, 19.5)cm.
Work first 2 rows of stripe pat with B.

BEG STRIPE PAT AND SHAPE RAGLAN CAP
Cont in St st and stripe pat, bind off 2 sts at beg of next 2 rows.
Dec row 1 (RS) K1, [SKP] twice, k to last 5 sts, [k2tog] twice, k1—4 sts dec'd.
Next row Purl.
Rep last 2 rows 1 (1, 0, 0) time more.
Dec row 2 (RS) K1, SKP, k to last 3 sts, k2tog, k1—2 sts dec'd.
Next row Purl.
Rep last 2 rows 7 (7, 10, 10) times more—8 (10, 11, 13) sts. Bind off.
Rep for 2nd sleeve.

Finishing
Weave in ends. Block pieces to measurements.
Sew raglan sleeves into raglan armholes of front and back. Sew side and sleeve

COLOR SWAP
When a patterns only uses the contrasting color for small details, such as the stripes in this sweater, you might be able to make a second one if you swap the colors.

seams.

COLLAR

With RS facing and circular needle and A, pick up and k 17 (20, 20, 22) sts from back neck edge, 7 (9, 10, 11) sts from top of left sleeve, 17 (20, 20, 22) sts from front neck edge, 7 (9, 10, 11) sts from top of right sleeve—48 (58, 60, 66) sts. Join and pm for beg of rnd.
Work in k1, p1 rib for 4 rnds. Bind off loosely in rib.
Weave in rem ends.

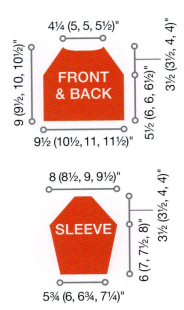

Pumpkin Spice Pullover

DESIGNED BY Cheryl Murray

Worked in the round up from their lower edges, the sleeves and body of this pullover are knit separately but then joined to complete a simple yet stunning colorwork yoke.

PULLOVER
Body
With A, using longer circular needle, cast on 172 (180, 188, 200, 212) sts. Join to work in rnds, taking care not to twist sts, pm for beg of rnd.
Purl 4 rnds.
Cont in St st (k every rnd) until piece measures 14½"/37cm from beg.
Lay piece aside.

Sleeves
With dpn and A, cast on 38 (40, 42, 44, 46) sts and divide over 4 dpn. Join, taking care not to twist sts, and pm for beg of rnd.
Purl 2 rnds.
Cont in St st until piece measures 2"/5cm from beg.

CHART 1
Cont in St st, work rnds 1–5 of chart 1. Cut B and C.

With A only, cont as foll:
Inc rnd K1, M1, k to 1 st before end of rnd, M1, k1.
Cont in St st, rep inc rnd every 6th (6th, 5th, 5th, 5th) rnd 14 (10, 16, 9, 5) times more, then every 0 (5th, 0, 4th, 4th) rnd 0 (5, 0, 9, 15) times—68 (72, 76, 82, 88) sts. Work even until piece measures 16¾"/42.5cm from beg.

Set aside and make a 2nd sleeve.
Yoke
K83 (87, 91, 97, 103) sts of body for front; place next 7 sts on scrap yarn for body's underarm; *place last 3 sts and first 4 sts of sleeve rnd (a total of 7 sts) on scrap yarn for sleeve's underarm; k rem 61 (65, 69, 75, 81) sts of sleeve*; k79 (83, 87, 93, 99) sts of body for back; place last 3 sts of back and first 4 sts of front (a total of 7 sts) on scrap yarn for body underarm; rep between *s once more—280 (296, 312, 336, 360) sts.
Join to work in rnds for yoke and pm for

SIZES
Small (Medium, Large, X-Large, XX-Large). Shown in size Small.

MEASUREMENTS
Bust 38 (40, 42, 44½, 47)"/96.5 (101.5, 106.5, 113, 119)cm
Length 24 (24, 24½, 25, 25½)"/61 (61, 62, 63.5, 64.5)cm
Upper arm 15 (16, 16¾, 18¼, 19½)"/38 (40.5, 42.5, 46.5, 49.5)cm

MATERIALS
- 3½oz/100g and 219yd/200m skein of any wool/viscose/nylon blend (4) 4 (5, 5, 6, 6) skeins in Gray (A) 1 skein each Beige (B) and Orange (C)
- One size 8 (5mm) circular needle, 16"/40cm long, *or size to obtain gauge*
- One size 8 (5mm) circular needle, 32"/80cm long
- One set (5) size 8 (5mm) double-pointed needles (dpn)
- Stitch markers
- Removable stitch marker
- Stitch holders
- Scrap yarn

GAUGE
18 sts and 26 rnds to 4"/10cm over St st using size 8 (5mm) needle.
TAKE TIME TO CHECK YOUR GAUGE.

NOTE
Pullover is worked in rounds in 3 separate pieces from the lower edge to the yoke. Then, the pieces are joined above the armhole and the yoke is worked in rounds to the neck edge.

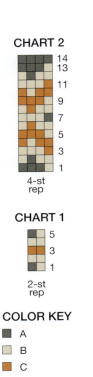

CHART 2

4-st rep

CHART 1

2-st rep

COLOR KEY
- A
- B
- C

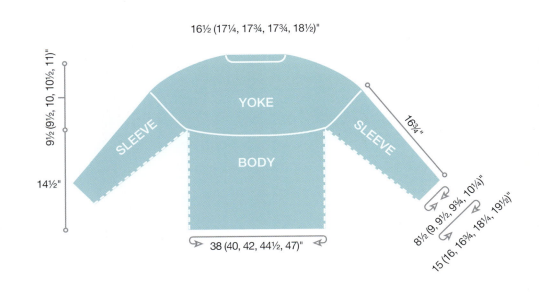

16½ (17¼, 17¾, 17¾, 18½)"

9½ (9½, 10, 10½, 11)"

SLEEVE

YOKE

SLEEVE

16¾"

14½"

BODY

38 (40, 42, 44½, 47)"

8½ (9, 9½, 9¾, 10¼)"

15 (16, 16¾, 18¼, 19½)"

beg of rnd. Knit 6 rnds.
Next dec rnd Dec 0 (1, 2, 1, 0) st(s) evenly around—280 (295, 310, 335, 360) sts.
Knit 7 (7, 7, 10, 10) rnds or until yoke measures 2¼ (2¼, 2¼, 2½, 2½)"/5.5 (5.5, 5.5, 6.5, 6.5)cm.
Dec rnd 1 *K3, k2tog; rep from * around—224 (236, 248, 268, 288) sts.
Work even in St st until yoke measures 4½ (4½, 4½, 5, 5)"/11.5 (11.5, 11.5, 12.5, 12.5)cm.
Dec rnd 2 *K2, k2tog; rep from * around—168 (177, 186, 201, 216) sts.
Knit 3 rnds.
Dec rnd 3 Knit, dec'ing 0 (1, 2, 1, 0) st(s) evenly around—168 (176, 184, 200, 216) sts.
Knit 0 (0, 3, 3, 3) rnds.

CHART 1
Cont in St st, work rnds 1-5 of chart 1. Cut B and C.

Cont with A only, knit 0 (0, 0, 0, 3) rnds.
Dec rnd 1 Knit, dec'ing 0 (2, 1, 2, 0) sts evenly spaced—168 (174, 183, 198, 216) sts.
Dec rnd 2 *K1, k2tog; rep from *

around—112 (116, 122, 132, 144) sts.

SIZE LARGE ONLY
Next dec rnd Knit, dec'ing 2 sts evenly spaced around—120 sts.

CHART 2 (ALL SIZES)
Cont in St st, work rnds 1-14 of chart 2.

Cut B and C.
Next dec rnd *K1, k2tog; rep from *, end k1 (2, 0, 0, 0)—75 (78, 80, 88, 96) sts.
Knit 0 (0, 0, 2, 2) rnds.

SIZES XL (XX-L) ONLY
Next dec rnd *K9 (6), k2tog; rep from * around—80 (84) sts.

ALL SIZES
Purl 2 rnds on rem 75 (78, 80, 80, 84) sts.
Bind off.

Finishing
Using Kitchener st over St st (see page 176), graft each set of 7 underarm sts of body and sleeves.
Weave in ends. Block lightly to measurements. ■

104

QUICK FINISH
This seamless construction requires minimal finishing. Graft a few stitches at each underarm, weave in some ends, block, and you're done!

Shawl-Collar Cardigan

DESIGNED BY Rosemary Drysdale

Narrow ribbed edges frame the Stockinette of this easy-fit cardigan. The front edges naturally roll inward for self-finishing and cushy edges.

SIZES
Sized for Small (Medium, Large, X-Large, 1X, 2X). Shown in size Medium.

MEASUREMENTS
Bust 40 (44, 47, 51, 56, 60)"/101.5 (111.5, 119.5, 129.5, 142, 152.5)cm
Length 25½ (26, 26½, 27, 27½, 28)"/64.5 (66, 67, 68.5, 69.5, 71)cm
Upper arm 12 (13, 14, 15, 16, 18)"/30.5 (33, 35.5, 38, 40.5, 45.5)cm

MATERIALS
- 3½oz/100g and 109yd/100m skein of any baby llama (5) 7 (8, 9, 10, 11, 12) skeins in White
- One pair size 9 (5.5mm) needles, *or size to obtain gauge*
- Stitch holders
- Pins

GAUGE
15 sts and 21 rows to 4"/10cm over St st using size 9 (5.5mm) needles.
TAKE TIME TO CHECK YOUR GAUGE.

CARDIGAN
Back
Cast on 61 (69, 75, 81, 91, 99) sts.
Row 1 (RS) K1, *p1, k1; rep from * to end.
Row 2 P1, *k1, p1; rep from * to end.
Rep last 2 rows for k1, p1 rib once more.
Inc row (RS) Cont rib over 5 sts, M1, k to last 5 sts, M1, cont rib over last 5 sts—2 sts inc'd.
Next row (WS) Cont rib over 5 sts, p to last 5 sts, cont rib over last 5 sts.
Rep last 2 rows 6 times more—75 (83, 89, 95, 105, 113) sts.
Cont in St st (k on RS, p on WS) over all sts until piece measures 17"/43cm from beg, end with a WS row.

SHAPE ARMHOLE
Cont in St st, bind off 3 (3, 4, 4, 5, 6) sts at beg of next 2 rows.
Dec row (RS) K2, ssk, k to last 4 sts, k2tog, k2—2 sts dec'd.
Purl 1 row.
Rep last 2 rows 3 (4, 4, 5, 5, 6) times more—61 (67, 71, 75, 83, 87) sts.
Work even until armhole measures 7½ (8, 8½, 9, 9½, 10)"/20.5 (21.5, 23, 24, 25.5)cm.

SHAPE SHOULDER
Cont in St st, bind off 6 (7, 7, 8, 9, 10) sts at beg of next 4 rows, then bind off 6 (7, 8, 8, 9, 9) sts at beg of next 2 rows. Bind off rem 25 (25, 27, 27, 29, 29) sts for back neck.

Left Front
Cast on 39 (43, 47, 49, 55, 59) sts.
Work 4 rows in k1, p1 rib same as for back.
Inc row (RS) Cont rib over 5 sts, M1, k to end—1 st inc'd.
Next row P to last 5 sts, cont rib over last 5 sts.
Rep last 2 rows 6 times more—46 (50, 54, 56, 62, 66) sts.
Cont in St st over all sts until piece measures 17"/43cm from beg, end with a WS row.

SHAPE ARMHOLE
Dec row 1 (RS) Bind off 3 (3, 4, 4, 5, 6) sts, k to end.
Purl 1 row.
Dec row 2 (RS) K2, ssk, k to end—1 st dec'd.
Purl 1 row.
Rep last 2 rows 3 (4, 4, 5, 5, 6) times more—39 (42, 45, 46, 51, 53) sts.
Work even until same length as back to shoulder.

SHAPE SHOULDER
Cont in St st, bind off from shoulder edge (beg of RS rows) 6 (7, 7, 8, 9, 10) sts twice, then 6 (7, 8, 8, 9, 9) sts once.
Place rem 21 (21, 23, 22, 24, 24) sts on a st holder.

Right Front
Cast on 39 (43, 47, 49, 55, 59) sts.
Work 4 rows in k1, p1 rib same as for back.
Inc row (RS) K to last 5 sts, M1, cont rib to end—1 st inc'd.
Next row Cont rib over 5 sts, p to end.
Rep last 2 rows 6 times more—46 (50, 54, 56, 62, 66) sts.
Cont in St st over all sts until piece

BLANK CANVAS Let simple Stockinette shine, or add color blocking, stripes, or embroidery. A variegated, tonal, speckled, or textured yarn could also make this classic look sing.

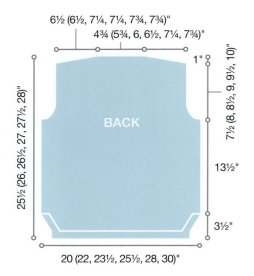
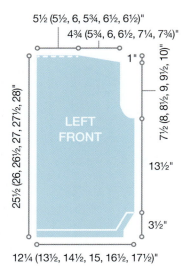
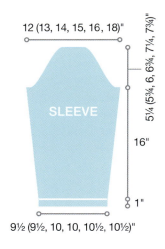

measures 17"/43cm from beg, end with a RS row.

SHAPE ARMHOLE
Dec row 1 (WS) Bind off 3 (3, 4, 4, 5, 6) sts, p to end.
Dec row 2 (RS) K to last 4 sts, k2tog, k2—1 st dec'd.
Purl 1 row.
Rep last 2 rows 3 (4, 4, 5, 5, 6) times more—39 (42, 45, 46, 51, 53) sts.
Work even until same length as back to shoulder.

SHAPE SHOULDER
Cont in St st, bind off from shoulder edge (beg of WS rows) 6 (7, 7, 8, 9, 10) sts twice, then 6 (7, 8, 8, 9, 9) sts once.
Place rem 21 (21, 23, 22, 24, 24) sts on a st holder.

Sleeves
Cast on 35 (35, 37, 37, 39, 39) sts.
Work 4 rows in k1, p1 rib same as for back.
Cont in St st as foll:
Work 8 rows even.
Inc row K2, M1, k to last 2 sts, M1, k2—2 sts inc'd.
Rep inc every 14th (10th, 8th, 6th, 6th, 4th) row 4 (6, 7, 9, 10, 13) times more—45 (49, 53, 57, 61, 67) sts.
Work even until piece measures 17"/43cm from beg, end with a WS row.

SHAPE CAP
Cont in St st, bind off 3 (3, 4, 4, 5, 6) sts at beg of next 2 rows.
Dec row (RS) K2, ssk, k to last 4 sts, k2tog, k2—2 sts dec'd. Purl 1 row.
Rep last 2 rows 11 (12, 13, 15, 16, 17) times more.
Bind off 3 (4, 4, 4, 4, 4) sts at beg of next 2 rows.
Bind off rem 9 (9, 9, 9, 9, 11) sts.
Work 2nd sleeve in same way.

Finishing
Weave in ends. Block pieces to measurements.
Align bound-off shoulder sts of fronts and back. Seam only bound-off sts tog for shoulder seams.

COLLAR
Place sts on left front holder onto needle and cont in St st until piece fits along one half of back neck bind-off for collar extension. Place sts on st holder.
Work sts from right front holder in same way.
Join collar extension sts using 3-needle bind-off (see page 173).
Seam sides of collar extension to back neck bind-off.

Pin sleeve caps into armholes with top center of sleeve caps at shoulder seams and edges of sleeve caps at first underarm bind-offs of body. Sew sleeves in place.

Sew sleeve seams.
Sew side seams, leaving the 5-st ribbed bands at lower edge unsewn.

Winter Haze Cardigan

DESIGNED BY Mari Lynn Patrick

This button-down cardigan sports an all-over texture pattern reminiscent of a hazy winter day. The cushy shawl collar is perfect for cozying up.

SIZES
Man's Small (Medium, Large, X-Large, XX-Large). Shown in size Medium.

MEASUREMENTS
Chest 38 (41, 44½, 48, 51)"/96.5 (104, 113, 122, 129.5)cm
Length (modern)* 26½ (27, 28, 29, 29½)"/67 (68.5, 71, 73.5, 75)cm
Length (traditional)* 28½ (29, 30, 31, 31½)"/72.5 (73.5, 76, 78.5, 80)cm
Upper arm 15½ (16, 17¼, 18½, 19)"/39.5 (40.5, 44, 47, 48)cm

*__Note__ The garment length is for a modern fit garment. For a traditional man's length, add 2"/5cm before the armhole shaping and an extra ball of yarn.

MATERIALS
- 3½oz/100g and 174yd/159m skeins of any wool (3)
  8 (8, 9, 10, 11) skeins in Variegated Brown
- One pair each sizes 8 and 10 (5 and 6mm) needles, *or size to obtain gauge*
- One size 8 (5mm) circular needle, 24"/60cm long
- Cable needle (cn)
- Stitch markers
- Six 1"/25mm buttons
- Sewing needle and thread to match yarn color

GAUGE
19 sts and 22 rows to 4"/10cm over chart pat using larger needles.
TAKE TIME TO CHECK YOUR GAUGE.

NOTES
1) The chart pattern has a cable that is worked (nontraditionally) on the wrong side rows to show up as a puckered stitch on the right side.

NOTES continued on page 112

CARDIGAN
Back
With smaller needles, cast on 90 (98, 106, 114, 122) sts.
Row 1 (RS) K2, *p2, k2; rep from * to end.
Cont in k2, p2 rib for 12 rows more.

BEGIN CHART
Change to larger needles.
Set-up row 1 (WS) Sl 1 wyif (selvage st), work 8-st rep of chart 11 (12, 13, 14, 15) times, p1 (selvage st).
Row 2 (RS) Sl 1 wyib (selvage st), work 8-st chart rep 11 (12, 13, 14, 15) times, k1 (selvage st).
Cont to foll chart in this way through row 9, then rep rows 2–9 until piece measures 16½"/42cm (modern fit) or 18½"/47cm (traditional fit) from beg.

SHAPE ARMHOLE
Cont in pat, bind off 5 sts at beg of next 2 rows.
Note When dec'ing in this section, work simple k2tog or p2tog on first or last 2 sts of chart pat depending on what the first block of sts are (knit or purl).
Dec 1 st each side of next 2 (3, 3, 5, 7) rows.
Work 1 row even.
Dec 1 st each side every RS row 0 (0, 2, 2, 3) times more—76 (82, 86, 90, 92) sts.
Work even until armhole measures 9 (9½, 10½, 11½, 12)"/23 (24, 26.5, 29, 30.5)cm. Pm on last WS row to mark center 24 (24, 26, 28, 30) sts.

SHAPE SHOULDER
Cont in pat, bind off 7 (8, 9, 8, 8) sts at beg of next 2 rows.
Next row (RS) Bind off 7 (8, 8, 9, 9) sts, work to center marked sts, join a 2nd ball of yarn and bind-off center marked sts, work to end.
Work both sides at once as foll:
Next row (WS) On first shoulder, bind off 7 (8, 8, 9, 9) sts, then work to end; on 2nd shoulder, work to end.
Next 2 rows On first shoulder, bind off 7 (8, 8, 9, 9) sts, then work to end; on 2nd shoulder, bind off 5 sts at neck edge, then work to end.

Right Front
With smaller needles, cast on 43 (47, 51, 55, 59) sts.
Row 1 (RS) Sl 1, k2, [p2, k2] 10 (11, 12, 13, 14) times.
Row 2 *P2, k2; rep from * to last 3 sts, p3.
Cont in k2, p2 rib as established for 11 rows more.

BEGIN CHART
Change to larger needles.
Set-up row 1 (WS) Sl 1 (selvage st), work 8-st chart rep 4 (5, 5, 6, 6) times, p3,

KEEPING TRACK
To keep track of how many increase/decrease rows you've worked, keep a tally in a notebook, mark up a copy of the pattern, or use a stitch/row counter. Figure out what works best for you so you know exactly where you are at all times.

NOTES continued from page 110

2) During increase or decrease sections, when there are 2 stitches at the end of cable row 5 or 9, work a 2-st LC, and when there are 3 sts, work a 2/1 LC.

3) When increasing or decreasing into pattern, use your preferred increase or decrease to result in a knit or purl stitch that fits into the pattern. Work to the inside of the selvage stitches.

STITCH GLOSSARY

4-st LC Sl 2 sts to cn and hold to *front*, k2, k2 from cn.
2-st LC Sl 1 st to cn and hold to *front*, k1, k1 from cn.
2/1 LC Sl 2 sts to cn and hold to *front*, k1, k2 from cn.

p2tog, k4 (0, 4, 0, 4), p1 (selvage st)—42 (46, 50, 54, 58) sts.
Row 2 (RS) Sl 1 wyib (selvage st), beg with st 1 (5, 1, 5, 1), work to end of 8-st rep, then work rep 4 (5, 5, 6, 6) times, k1 (selvage st). Cont to foll chart in this way through row 9, then rep rows 2-9 until piece measures 16½"/42cm (modern fit) or 18½"/47cm (traditional fit) from beg, end with a RS row.

SHAPE ARMHOLE

Cont in pat, bind off 5 sts from armhole edge (beg of WS row) once.
Work 1 row even.
Then, dec 1 st at armhole edge every row 2 (3, 3, 5, 7) times—35 (38, 42, 44, 46) sts.
Then, dec 1 st at armhole edge every WS row 0 (0, 2, 2, 3) times more—35 (38, 40, 42, 43) sts.
Work 3 (3, 5, 5, 5) rows even.

SHAPE V-NECK

Dec row (RS) Sl 1, dec 1 st in pat, work pat to end.
Cont in pat, rep dec row every RS row 6 (6, 8, 9, 10) times more, then every 4th row 7 (7, 6, 6, 6) times, AT THE SAME TIME, when armhole measures same as back, shape shoulders by binding off 7 (8, 9, 8, 8) sts from shoulder edge at beg of next 3 WS rows.

Left Front

With smaller needles, cast on 43 (47, 51, 55, 59) sts.
Row 1 (RS) *K2, p2; rep from * to last 3 sts, k3.
Row 2 Sl 1, p2, [k2, p2] 10 (11, 12, 13, 14) times.
Cont in k2, p2 ribs as established for 11 rows more.

BEGIN CHART

Change to larger needles.
Set-up row 1 (WS) Sl 1 (selvage st), p4 (0, 4, 0, 4), k3, k2tog, work 8-st chart rep 4 (5, 5, 6, 6) times, p1 (selvage st)—42 (46, 50, 54, 58) sts.
Row 2 (RS) Sl 1 wyib (selvage st), beg with st 1 (5, 1, 5, 1), work to end of 8-st rep, then work rep 4 (5, 5, 6, 6) times, k1 (selvage st). Cont to foll chart in this way through row 9, then rep rows 2-9 until piece measures 16½"/42cm (modern fit) or 18½"/47cm (traditional fit) from beg, end with a WS row.

SHAPE ARMHOLE

Cont in pat, bind off 5 sts from armhole edge (beg of RS row) once.
Work 1 row even.
Then, dec 1 st at armhole edge every row 2 (3, 3, 5, 7) times—35 (38, 42, 44, 46) sts.
Then, dec 1 st at armhole edge every RS row 0 (0, 2, 2, 3) times more—35 (38, 40, 42, 43) sts.
Work 3 (3, 5, 5, 5) rows even.

SHAPE V-NECK

Dec row (WS) Sl 1, dec 1 st in pat, work pat to end.
Rep dec row every WS row 6 (6, 8, 9, 10) times more, every 4th row 7 (7, 6, 6, 6) times, AT THE SAME TIME, when armhole measures same as back, shape shoulders by binding off 7 (8, 9, 8, 8) sts from shoulder edge at beg of next 3 RS rows.

Sleeves

With smaller needles, cast on 50 (54, 58, 62, 66) sts.
Work in k2, p2 rib same as for back for 13 rows.

BEGIN CHART

Change to larger needles.
Set-up row 1 (WS) Sl 1 wyif (selvage st), work 8-st rep 6 (6, 7, 7, 8) times, p0 (4, 0, 4, 0), p1 (selvage st).
Row 2 (RS) Sl 1 wyib (selvage st), beg with st 1 (5, 1, 5, 1), work to end of 8-st rep, then work rep 5 (6, 6, 7, 7) times, k1 (selvage st). Cont to foll chart in this way through row 9, then rep rows 2-9, AT THE SAME TIME, inc 1 st each side on the 4th chart row,

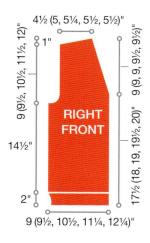
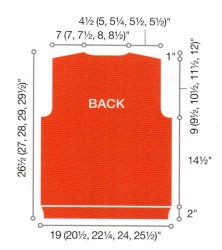

then every 8th row 10 (11, 10, 9, 12) times more, then every 6th row 2 (0, 2, 4, 0) times—76 (78, 84, 90, 92) sts.
Work even until piece measures 19½ (19½, 20, 20½, 20½)"/ 49.5 (49.5, 51, 52, 52)cm from beg.

SHAPE CAP
Cont in pat, bind off 5 sts at beg of next 2 rows.
Dec 1 st each side every RS row 11 (12, 15, 18, 19) times—44 sts.
Bind off 4 sts at beg of next 4 rows.
Bind off 28 sts.
Work 2nd sleeve in same way.

Right Front Band
With smaller needles and RS facing, pick up and k 51 (53, 57, 59, 61) sts evenly along the center front straight edge.
Inc row 1 (WS) K1, [pfb, kfb] 24 (25, 27, 28, 29) times, pfb, p1—100 (104, 112, 116, 120) sts.
Row 2 (RS) K3, *p2, k2; rep from * to last st, p1.
Cont in k2, p2 rib for 6 rows more. Then, to stabilize the edge, bind off as foll:
Bind-off row (WS) *Bind off 2 sts, k2tog and bind off; rep from * to end.

Left Front Band
Work as for right front band for 4 rows.

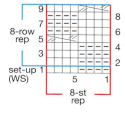

STITCH KEY
☐ k on RS, p on WS
⊟ p on RS, k on WS
▧ 4-st LC

Buttonhole row (WS) Rib 4 (8, 8, 5, 8), *bind off 2 sts, rib 16 (16, 18, 19, 19) more sts; rep from *, bind off 2 sts, work 4 (4, 2, 4, 5) sts.
On next row, work in rib and cast on 2 sts over each set of bound-off sts.
Finish same as for right front band.

Finishing
Weave in ends. Block pieces to measurements.

Collar
Align shoulder edges of back and front pieces. Sew shoulder seams.
With RS facing and circular needle, pick up and k 22 (22, 22, 24, 24) sts along right front neck edge, pm, pick up and k 40 (40, 40, 43, 46) sts from back neck, pm, and then pick up and k 22 (22, 22, 24, 24) sts from left front neck edge.
Set-up inc row (WS) Pfb, kfb, [pfb, kfb] 10 (10, 10, 11, 11) times, sm, [p2, kfb] 13 (13, 13, 14, 15) times, pfb, sm, [kfb, pfb] 10 (10, 10, 11, 11) times, kfb, pfb—142 (142, 142, 154, 158) sts.
Short-row 1 (RS) K2, *p2, k2; rep from * to last 4 sts, turn.
Short-row 2 Sl 1, work in rib to last 4 sts, turn.
Short-row 3 Work in rib to 4 sts before previous turn, turn work.
Short-rows 4–20 Rep short-row 3.
Next 2 rows Work to end of entire row.
Work 5 rows more. Bind off all sts. (Do *not* work the k2tog as on the front bands).

Finishing
Pin sleeve caps into armholes with top center of sleeve caps at shoulder seams and edges of sleeve caps at first underarm bind-offs of body. Sew sleeves in place.
Sew side and sleeve seams.
Weave in rem ends.
Sew on buttons opposite buttonholes.

Buttoned Poncho Cardigan

DESIGNED BY Cheryl Murray

The perfect poncho/cardigan hybrid, wear this garment with just the sides, just the fronts, or everything buttoned up. The cushy stitch pattern makes it a cozy delight no matter how you wear it.

MEASUREMENTS
Bust 52"/109cm
Length 26"/66cm

MATERIALS
- 3½oz/100g and 219yd/109m skein of any wool (5)
  8 skeins in Beige
- One pair size 11 (7mm) needles, *or size to obtain gauge*
- One size 10½" (6.5mm) circular needle, 32"/80cm long
- Stitch holder
- Six 13/8"/34mm buttons
- Sewing needle and thread to match yarn

GAUGES
14 sts and 20 rows to 4"/10cm over textured rib using larger needles.
TAKE TIME TO CHECK YOUR GAUGE.

NOTES
1) Body of poncho is worked in one piece, beginning with the back. At the shoulder, the fronts continue in two separate pieces to the lower front edges.
2) The One-Row Buttonhole method is used to create a neat buttonhole. The traditional buttonhole (bind off 3 sts on one row, then cast on 3 sts on following row) can be used instead, if desired.

TEXTURED RIB
(an odd number of sts)
Row 1 (RS) *K1, p1; rep from * to last st, k1.
Row 2 *P1, k1; rep from * to last st, p1.
Rows 3 and 4 Knit.
Rep rows 1–4 for textured rib.

K2, P2 RIB
(multiple of 4 sts plus 2)
Row 1 (RS) *K2, p2; rep from * to last 2 sts, k2.
Row 2 *P2, k2; rep from * to last 2 sts, p2.
Rep rows 1 and 2 for k2, p2 rib.

ONE-ROW BUTTONHOLE
1) Wyif sl 1, bring yarn to back between needles and drop yarn, sl 1, pass first slipped st over 2nd slipped st to bind off first st; [sl 1, pass previous st over last slipped st to bind off] twice; sl last slipped st to LH needle, turn work.
2) Bring yarn between needles to back of work, cast on 4 sts using cable cast-on (see page 168); turn work.
3) Sl 1 st, pass last cast-on st over slipped st as if to bind off; return slipped st to LH needle.
Buttonhole is complete.

PONCHO CARDIGAN
Back
With larger needles, cast on 85 sts.
Work in textured rib for 28"/71cm, end with a pat row 3.
Next row (WS) K29 and place these sts on a st holder, bind off next 27 sts, k to end.

Right Front
Cont in textured rib over rem 29 sts on needle for 2 rows more.
Inc row (RS) Work in pat to last st, M1, k1—1 st inc'd.
Rep inc every other row once more, then every 4th row 10 times, working inc sts into rib pat—41 sts.
Work even in pat until piece measures 28"/71cm from neck bind-off. Bind off in pat.

Left Front
Place sts on st holder onto needle. With RS facing, work 2 rows even in pat.
Inc row (RS) K1, M1, work in pat to end—1 st inc'd.

BUTTON, BUTTON
Bright or neutral. Ornate metal or smooth plastic. Rustic wood or varnished wood. The buttons you choose affect the overall vibe of a garment.

Rep inc row every other row once more, then every 4th row 10 times, working inc sts into rib pat—41 sts.
Work even in pat until piece measures 28"/71cm from neck bind-off.
Bind off in pat.

Finishing

LEFT SIDE BUTTON BAND

With RS facing and circular needle, beg at lower side (arm) edge of left front, pick up and k 99 sts along left front and 99 sts along side of left back—198 sts.
Work 3 rows in k2, p2 rib.
Buttonholes row (RS) Work 13 st in pat, work one-row buttonhole, work 13 sts in pat, work one-row buttonhole, work in pat to end.
Work 3 rows more in k2, p2 rib. Bind off in pat.

RIGHT SIDE BUTTON BAND

With RS facing and circular needle, beg at lower side (arm) edge of right back, pick up and k 99 sts along side of right back and 99 sts along side of right front—198 sts.
Work 3 rows in k2, p2 rib.
Buttonholes row (RS) Work 167 sts in pat, work one-row buttonhole, work 13 sts in pat, work one-row buttonhole, work in pat to end.
Work 3 rows more in k2, p2 rib. Bind off in pat.

COLLAR

With RS facing and circular needle, beg at last inc row on right front, pick up and k 36 sts along right neck edge, 27 sts along back neck edge, 36 sts along left neck edge, end at last shaping row on right left—99 sts.
Work in k2, p2 rib for 1 row, dec'ing 1 st at center back—98 sts

Shape collar

Short-row 1 (RS) Work rib to last 34 sts, w&t (see page 174).
Short-row 2 (WS) Work rib to last 34 sts, w&t.
Short-row 3 (RS) Work rib to last 32 sts, w&t.
Short row 4 (WS) Work rib to last 32 sts, w&t.
Cont to work short-rows in this way, working 2 more sts at end of every row, until 6 sts each side rem unworked, then work 3 more sts at end of every row until all sts have been worked.
Work even in k2, p2 rib over all sts until collar measures 8"/20.5cm at back neck. Bind off loosely in pat.

LEFT FRONT BUTTON BAND

With RS facing and circular needle, pick up and k 62 sts evenly along left front edge.
Work in k2, p2 rib for 7 rows. Bind off in pat.

RIGHT FRONT BUTTONHOLE BAND

With RS facing and circular needle, pick up and k 62 sts evenly along right front edge.
Work in k2, p2 rib for 3 rows.
Buttonhole row (RS) Work 41 sts, work one-row buttonhole, work 13 sts, work one-row buttonhole, work to end.
Work rib for 2 rows more. Bind off in pat.

Weave in ends.
Sew buttons on left front button band opposite buttonholes.
Sew buttons on back side edgings opposite buttonholes on front sides.
Seam side edges of collar to top of front bands.

Perforated Cardigan

DESIGNED BY Cheryl Murray

Knit mainly in easy Stockinette stitch, this cardigan sports textural features such as garter eyelet bands, deep garter stitch cuffs, and front pockets.

SIZES
Small (Medium, Large, X-Large, XX-Large). Shown in size Small.

MEASUREMENTS
Bust (closed) 41 (43½, 46, 48, 50)"/104 (110.5, 117, 122, 127)cm
Length 25 (25½, 26, 26½, 27)"/63.5 (64.5, 66, 67, 68.5)cm
Upper arm 18 (19, 20, 21, 22)"/45.5 (48, 51, 53, 56)cm

MATERIALS
- 1¾oz/50g and 114yd/104m skein of any wool ③ 14 (15, 17, 18, 19) skeins in Gray
- One pair size 6 (4mm) needles, *or size to obtain gauge*
- One size 6 (4mm) circular needle, 32"/80cm long
- Removable stitch markers
- Stitch holders

GAUGE
21 sts and 30 rows to 4"/10cm over St st using size 6 (4mm) needles.
TAKE TIME TO CHECK YOUR GAUGE.

EYELET PATTERN
(even number of sts)
Row 1 (WS) Knit.
Row 2 (RS) *K2tog, yo; rep from * to last 2 sts, k2.
Row 3 Knit.
These 3 rows form eyelet pat.

CARDIGAN
Back
Cast on 112 (118, 124, 130, 136) sts.
Work in garter st (k every row) for 1"/2.5cm.
Cont in St st (k on RS, p on WS) until piece measures 8"/20.5cm from beg, end with a WS row.
Dec row (RS) K1, k2tog, k to last 3 sts, ssk, k1—2 sts dec'd.
Work even until piece measures 15"/38cm from beg, end with a WS row.
Rep dec row on next RS row—108 (114, 120, 126, 132) sts.
Work even in St st until piece measures 16"/40.5cm from beg.
Pm on sts at each side of next row to mark beg of armholes.
Work even in St St until piece measures 7½ (8, 8½, 9, 9½)"/19 (20.5, 21.5, 23, 24)cm from armhole markers.

SHAPE NECK
Next row (RS) K32 (35, 38, 40, 43), join a 2nd ball of yarn and bind off center 44 (44, 44, 46, 46) sts, k to end.
Cont in St st, working both sides as foll:
Next dec row (WS) For first shoulder, p all sts; for 2nd shoulder, bind off 2 sts, p to end.
Next dec row (RS) For first shoulder, k all sts; for 2nd shoulder, bind off 2 sts, k to end.
Next dec row (WS) For first shoulder, p all sts; for 2nd shoulder, bind off 1 st, p to end.
Next dec row (RS) For first shoulder, k all sts; for 2nd shoulder, bind off 1 st, k to end—29 (32, 35, 37, 40) sts rem each side.
Work even over both sides until armholes measure 9 (9½, 10, 10½, 11)"/23 (24, 25.5, 26.5, 28)cm from armhole markers. Place sts each side on separate st holders.

Left Front
Cast on 47 (50, 53, 56, 59) sts.
Work in garter st for 1"/2.5cm.
Cont in St st until piece measures 8"/20.5cm from beg.

POSSIBLE POCKETS
The pockets in this cardigan are added after the fronts are knitted. You can easily leave them off.

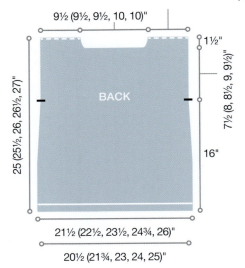
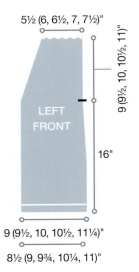
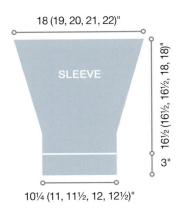

Dec row (RS) K1, k2tog, k to end—1 st dec'd.
Work even until piece measures 15"/38cm from beg.
Rep dec row on next RS row—45 (48, 51, 54, 57) sts.
Work even until piece measures 16"/40.5cm from beg. Pm on st at beg of RS row to mark beg of armhole.

SHAPE NECK
Dec row (RS) K to last 3 sts, ssk, k1—1 st dec'd.
Cont in St st, rep dec row every other row twice more, then every 4th row 13 (13, 13, 14, 14) times—29 (32, 35, 37, 40) sts.
Work even until armhole measures 9 (9½, 10, 10½, 11)"/23 (24, 25.5, 26.5, 28)cm from armhole marker.
Place sts for back left shoulder on needle. Hold RS of left front and back tog, use 3-needle bind-off (see page 173) to join shoulder sts.

Right Front
Work same as for left front until piece measures 8"/20.5cm from beg, end with a WS row.
Dec row (RS) K to last 3 sts, ssk, k1—1 st dec'd.

Work even until piece measures 15"/38cm from beg.
Rep dec row on next RS row—45 (48, 51, 54, 57) sts.
Work even until piece measures 16"/40.5cm from beg. Pm on st at end of RS row to mark beg of armhole.

SHAPE NECK
Dec row (RS) K1, k2tog, k to end—1 st dec'd.
Cont in St st, rep dec row every other row twice more, then every 4th row 13 (13, 13, 14, 14) times—29 (32, 35, 37, 40) sts.
Work even until armhole measures 9 (9½, 10, 10½, 11)"/23 (24, 25.5, 26.5, 28)cm from armhole marker.
Place sts for back right shoulder on needle. Hold RS of right front and back tog, use 3-needle bind-off (see page 173) to join shoulder sts.

Sleeves
Cast on 54 (58, 60, 64, 66) sts.
Work in garter st for 3"/7.5cm.
Dec row (RS) Knit, dec'ing 4 (4, 4, 6, 6) sts evenly spaced—50 (54, 56, 58, 60) sts.
Cont in St st until piece measures 6½"/16.5cm from beg.

Note Read before cont to knit.
Inc row (RS) K1, M1, k to last st, M1, k1.
Rep inc row every 4th row 22 (22, 24, 25, 27) times more AT THE SAME TIME when piece measures 10"/25.5cm from beg, end with a RS row and then work 3-row eyelet pat over next 3 rows.
Cont in St st and rep inc row as established, rep 3-row eyelet pat again after piece measures 14 (14, 14, 15, 15)"/35.5 (35.5, 35.5, 38, 38)cm from beg and then again when piece measures 19 (19, 19, 20½, 20½)"/48 (48, 48, 52, 52)cm from beg.
After inc's and 3rd set of eyelet pat rows are completed, bind off all 96 (100, 106, 110, 116) sts knitwise on a RS row.
Work 2nd sleeve in same way.

Left Pocket
Cast on 35 sts.
Work in St st for 6"/15cm, end with a WS row.
Cont in St st, bind off 5 sts at beg of next 7 RS rows. Cut yarn.
With RS facing, pick up and k 35 sts along shaped bound-off edge.
Work in garter st for 1"/2.5cm. Bind off.

Right Pocket

Cast on 35 sts.
Work in St st for 6"/15cm, end with a RS row.
Cont in St st, bind off 5 sts at beg of next 7 WS rows. Cut yarn.
With RS facing, pick up and k 35 sts along shaped bound-off edge.
Work in garter st for 1"/2.5cm. Bind off.

Finishing

Sew pockets in place to fronts at top of garter bands and even with center front edges.

FRONT AND NECKBAND

With RS facing and using larger circular needle, pick up and k 136 (139, 142, 144, 147) sts from right front edge, 55 (55, 55, 57, 57) sts from back neck edge, and 136 (139, 142, 144, 147) sts from left front edge—327 (333, 339, 345, 351) sts.
Knit 9 rows.
Next row (RS) *K2tog, yo; rep from * to last st, k1.
Knit 8 rows. Bind off knitwise.

With center of bound-off sts of sleeve at shoulder seam, sew sleeves to armholes between markers.
Sew side seams.
Sew sleeve seams, sewing garter cuffs so seam is on RS when cuff is folded back.
Weave in ends. Block to measurements.

Summer Cardigan

DESIGNED BY Cheryl Murray

A lacy cardigan with minimal shaping provides an easy and fun knit. The roomy fit is extra comfy when in need of just a little extra warmth during the warmer months.

SIZES
Small (Medium, Large, X-Large, XX-Large). Shown in size Small.

MEASUREMENTS
Bust (closed) 42 (46, 50, 54, 57)"/106.5 (117, 127, 137, 144.5)cm
Length 28 (28½, 29, 29½, 30)"/71 (72.5, 73.5, 75, 76)cm
Upper arm 17 (18, 19, 20, 21)"/43 (45.5, 48, 51, 53)cm

MATERIALS
- 1¾oz/50g and 109yd/100m skeins of any cotton (4)
  11 (11, 12, 13, 14) skeins in Pink
- One pair size 7 (4.5mm) needles, *or size to obtain gauge*
- One size 7 (4.5mm) circular needle, 32"/80cm long
- Removable stitch markers

GAUGE
17 sts and 25 rows to 4"/10cm over lace rib pat using size 7 (4.5mm) needles.
TAKE TIME TO CHECK YOUR GAUGE.

NOTE
When working a yarn over before a purl stitch, bring yarn to front between needles, bring yarn over needle to back, and then bring yarn to front between needles again, making a complete circle around the needle.

TEXTURED RIB
(an odd number of sts)
Row 1 (RS) *K1, p1; rep from * to last st, k1.
Row 2 *P1, k1; rep from * to last st, p1.
Rows 3 and 4 Knit.
Rep rows 1–4 for textured rib.

K2, P2 RIB
(multiple of 4 sts plus 2)
Row 1 (RS) *K2, p2; rep from * to last 2 sts, k2.
Row 2 *P2, k2; rep from * to last 2 sts, p2.
Rep rows 1 and 2 for k2, p2 rib.

SLOPED BIND-OFF
1) One row before next bind-off row, work to last st of row. Do not work this st. Turn work.
2) Wyib, sl first st from left needle purlwise.
3) Pass unworked st of previous row over slipped st to bind off first st. Cont to bind off desired number of sts for that row. Work to end of row.
Rep steps 1–3 until bind-off is complete.

LACE RIB PATTERN
(multiple of 4 sts plus 2 selvage sts)
Row 1 (RS) K1, *yo, SK2P, yo, p1; rep from * to last st, k1.
Row 2 P1, *k1, p3; rep from * to last st, p1.
Row 3 K1, *k3, p1; rep from * to last st, k1.
Row 4 Rep row 2.
Rep 1–4 rows for lace rib pat.

CARDIGAN
Back
Cast on 90 (98, 106, 114, 122) sts.
Row 1 (RS) K2, *p1, k1; rep from * to end.
Row 2 *P1, k1; rep from * to last 2 sts, p2.
Rep rows 1 and 2 once more.

Work in lace rib pat until piece measures 17½"/44.5cm from beg. Pm on st at each side of last row to mark beg of armholes. Cont in pat, work even until piece measures 8½ (9, 9½, 10, 10½)"/21.5 (23, 24, 25.5, 26.5)cm from markers, end with a WS row.

SUMMER KNITS
Wearing knits isn't just for the fall and winter. Knits made with cotton yarn can be light and perfect for warmer weather, especially when in a mesh pattern, as seen here.

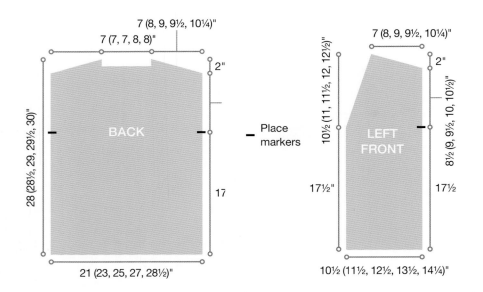
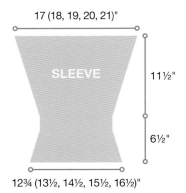

SHAPE SHOULDERS AND NECK
Cont in pat and using sloped bind-off, bind off 5 (5, 7, 6, 8) sts at beg of next 8 (4, 4, 4, 4) rows, then 0 (6, 6, 7, 7) sts at beg of next 4 rows—50 (54, 54, 62, 62) sts.
Pm on st each side of center 30 (30, 30, 34, 34) sts on last WS row.
Next row (RS) Bind off 5 (6, 6, 7, 7) sts, work to center marked sts, join a 2nd ball of yarn and bind off center 30 (30, 30, 34, 34) sts, work to end.
Cont in pat and working both sides at once, bind off 5 (6, 6, 7, 7) sts at beg (shoulder edge) of next 3 rows to complete shoulders.

Left Front
Cast on 45 (49, 53, 57, 61) sts.
Row 1 (RS) K2, *p1, k1; rep from* to last 2 sts, k2.
Row 2 P2, *k1, p1; rep from * to last 2 sts, p2.
Rep rows 1 and 2 once more, inc'ing 1 st at end of last WS row—46 (50, 54, 58, 62) sts.

Work in lace rib pat until piece measures 17½"/44.5cm from beg, end with a WS row. Pm
to mark beg of armhole at beg of next RS row.

SHAPE NECK
Note When working neck shaping, to keep in pat, work only (SKP, yo) or yo, SKP instead of yo, SK2P, yo when 2nd yo is eliminated in dec or work only a k1 (or p1) when there are not sufficient sts for pat.
Dec row (RS) Work in pat to last 3 sts, k2tog, k1—1 st dec'd.
Cont in pat, rep dec row every 4th row 15 (15, 15, 17, 17) times more—30 (34, 38, 40, 44) sts.
Work even until armhole measures same as back from marker to shoulder shaping.

SHAPE SHOULDER
Cont in pat, bind off 5 (5, 7, 6, 8) sts from shoulder edge (beg of RS rows) twice, then 5 (6, 6, 7, 7) sts 4 times.

Right Front
Cast on 46 (50, 54, 58, 62) sts.
Row 1 (RS) K2, *p1, k1; rep from *, to end.
Row 2 *P1, k1; rep from * to last 2 sts, p2.
Rep rows 1 and 2 once more.

Work in lace rib pat until piece measures 17½"/44.5cm from beg, end with a WS row. Pm to mark beg of armhole at end of next RS row.

SHAPE NECK
Dec row (RS) K1, SKP, work in pat to end—1 st dec'd.
Rep dec row every 4th row 15 (15, 15, 17, 17) times more—30 (34, 38, 40, 44) sts.
Work even until armhole measures same as back from marker to shoulder shaping.

SHAPE SHOULDER
Cont in pat, bind off 5 (5, 7, 6, 8) sts from shoulder edge (beg of WS rows) twice, then 5 (6, 6, 7, 7) sts 4 times.

Sleeves
Cast on 54 (58, 62, 66, 70) sts.
Row 1 (RS) K2, *p1, k1; rep from * to end.
Row 2 *P1, k1; rep from * to last 2 sts, p2.
Rep rows 1 and 2 once more.

Work in lace rib pat for 6 rows.
Dec row (RS) SKP, work to last 2 sts, k2tog—2 sts dec'd.
Rep dec row every 12th row twice more—48 (52, 56, 60, 64) sts.

Cont in pat, work even until piece measures 6½"/16.5cm from beg, end with a WS row.

Inc row (RS) K1, M1, work to last st, M1, k1—2 sts inc'd.

Cont in pat, rep inc row every 4th row 13 times more, then every 6th row once—78 (82, 86, 90, 94) sts.

Work even until piece measures 18"/45.5cm from beg. Bind off.

Finishing
Weave in ends. Block pieces lightly to measurements.

Sew shoulder seams. Set sleeves into armholes between markers, easing in to fit if necessary.
Sew side and sleeve seams.

FRONT AND NECKBAND
With RS facing and using circular needle, pick up and k 80 sts along right front edge to neck shaping, 51 (53, 55, 58, 60) sts along shaped right front neck edge, 41 (41, 41, 45, 45) sts along shaped back neck edge, 51 (53, 55, 58, 60) sts along shaped left front neck edge, and 80 sts along left front—303 (307, 311, 321, 325) sts.

Row 1 (WS) P1, *k1, p1; rep from * to end.
Row 2 K1, *p1, k1; rep from * to end.
Rep rows 1 and 2 for k1, p1 rib for 5 rows more.
Bind off loosely knitwise.
Weave in rem ends.

Garter-Stitch Baby Cardigan

DESIGNED BY Jacqueline van Dillen

Multi-directional garter stitch, squishy and soft, is perfect for baby in this cardigan. A shawl collar and rolled cuffs add the cuteness.

SIZES
Sized for 0–6 months (12 months, 18 months, 24 months). Shown in size 12 months.

MEASUREMENTS
Chest (closed) 20½ (23, 24½, 26½)"/52 (58.5, 62, 67)cm
Length 11¼ (12, 12¾, 14)"/28.5 (30.5, 32.5, 35.5)cm
Upper arm 8½ (9, 9½, 10)"/21.5 (23, 24, 25.5)cm

MATERIALS
- 1 ¾oz/50g and 136yd/124m skein of any wool (3)
  4 (4, 5, 6) skeins in Gray
- One pair size 5 (3.75mm) needles, *or size to obtain gauge*
- One extra size 5 (3.75mm) needle
- One size 5 (3.75mm) double-pointed needle (dpn)
- Stitch holders
- Removable stitch markers
- Three 11/16"/18mm buttons

GAUGE
22 sts and 44 rows to 4"/10cm over garter st using size 5 (3.75mm) needles. *TAKE TIME TO CHECK YOUR GAUGE.*

NOTE
Jacket is constructed by working from cuff to cuff and splitting at the neck edge to work the front and back separately, then finished at the center back. After joining the 2 sleeve segments at the center back, the body is worked downwards by picking up stitches along the garter ridges. The lower edge is finished with an I-cord bind-off.

CARDIGAN
Right Sleeve
Beg at cuff edge, cast on 36 (40, 42, 44) sts.
Work in garter st (k every row) for 16 rows.
Inc row (RS) K1, kfb, k to last 2 sts, kfb, k1—2 sts inc'd.
Cont in garter st, rep inc row every 14th (16th, 18th, 18th) row 5 times more—48 (52, 54, 56) sts.
Work even until piece measures 8 (9, 10½, 11½)"/20.5 (23, 26.5, 29)cm from beg and there are 88 (100, 116, 126) rows or 44 (50, 58, 63) ridges.
Pm on st at each side of last row worked to indicate end of sleeve side seam.
Work even after sleeve markers for 34 (40, 44, 50) rows, which is 17 (20, 22, 25) garter ridges.

SEPARATE FOR FRONT AND BACK
Next row (RS) K24 (26, 27, 28) for front, bind off 2 sts, k22 (24, 25, 26) for back. Place front sts on st holder and work back sts first.

Right Back
Knit 24 rows (12 garter ridges) over 22 (24, 25, 26) back sts.
Place sts on a st holder for finishing at center back later.

Right Front
Place 24 (26, 27, 28) sts of front onto needle. With WS facing, cast on 12 sts (to fit across one half of straight back neck edge), k to end—36 (38, 39, 40) sts.
Cont in garter st on these sts for a total of 30 rows (15 garter ridges).
Bind off on WS. These rows form center front shawl collar.

Left Sleeve
Work same as for right sleeve up to separate for front and back.

SEPARATE FOR FRONT AND BACK
Next row (RS) K22 (24, 25, 26) for back, bind off 2 sts, k24 (26, 27, 28) for front. Place back sts on st holder and work front sts first.

Left Front
K24 (26, 27, 28) front sts, turn work, and cast on 12 sts (to fit across one half of straight back neck edge).
Cont in garter st on these sts for a total of 32 rows (16 ridges). Bind off on WS.

Left Back
Place 22 (24, 25, 26) sts of back onto needle. With WS facing, join yarn. Knit 24 rows (or 12 ridges).

Join Back
With RS of right and front backs held tog, join using 3-needle bind-off (see page 173) to form center back seam.

EVERY WHICH WAY

Knits that grow from multiple directions, such as this one, can be a lot of fun. Take things one step at a time and marvel at how things shape up.

Sew sides of shawl collar extensions from fronts along center back neck edge. Sew bound-off edges of shawl collar extensions tog at center back neck. Sew sleeve seams from cuffs to markers. Yoke is now complete.

Body

With RS facing and beg at left front center edge, pick up and k 1 st for every garter ridge along bottom edge of yoke—122 (134, 142, 154) sts.

Row 1 (WS) Sl 2 wyif, k to last 2 sts, sl 2 wyif.
Row 2 Knit.
Row 3 Sl 2 wyif, k to last 2 sts, sl 2 wyif.
Buttonhole row 4 (RS) K to last 7 sts, [yo] twice, k2tog, k to end.
Row 5 Sl 2 wyif, k to double yo, k1 into first yo, k1 tbl into 2nd yo, k to last 2 sts, sl 2 wyif
[Rep rows 2 and 3 five times more, rep row 2 once more, then rep buttonhole row 4 and row 5 once more] twice—3 buttonholes total.
Rep rows 2 and 3 until body measures 7 (7½, 8, 9)"/18 (19, 20.5, 23)cm from pick-up row. Do not bind off.

Finishing
I-CORD BIND-OFF

With RS facing, use a dpn to cast on 2 sts onto knitting needle. Using knitting needle as LH needle and dpn as RH needle, work as foll:
Row 1 (RS) K1, k2tog, sl both sts to LH needle, bring yarn around back to work next from RS.
Rep row 1 until 2 sts rem, K2tog. Fasten off.

Sew buttons opposite buttonholes. Weave in ends.

RIDGE PATTERN
Row 1 (RS) K1, k2tog, k to end.
Row 2 K1, p to last 3 sts, p2tog, k1.
Row 3 K1, k2tog, k to end.
Ridge row 4 Knit.
Rep rows 1–4 until 2 sts rem.
Bind off.

Finishing
Weave in ends.
Block to measurements.

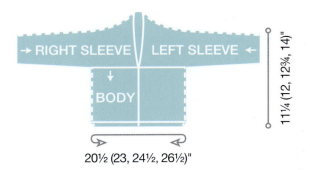

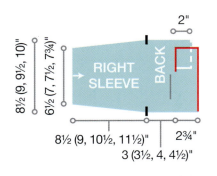

Garter Stripes Blanket

DESIGNED BY Sandi Prosser

Worked in halves in two different directions, this blanket features wide black and white stripes in garter stitch. A bonus block in black and white and stripes makes for a great toy.

BLANKET
Increasing Sequence
With circular needle and A, cast on 1 st. Work in garter st (k every row) and stripe sequence as foll:
Inc row 1 (RS) Kfb—2 sts.
Inc row 2 Kfb, k1—3 sts.
Inc row 3 K1, M1, k to end of row—1 st inc'd.
Cont stripe sequence and rep row 3 until there are 231 sts on needle, end with a WS row.
Inc row (RS) With A, k1, M1, k to end of row—232 sts.

Short-Row Mitered Sequence
INCREASING EDGE
Row 1 (WS) With A, k1, M1, SKP, turn.
Rows 2, 4, 6, and 8 K to end of row.
Row 3 K1, M1, k1, SKP, turn.
Row 5 K1, M1, k2, SKP, turn.
Row 7 K1, M1, k3, SKP, turn.
Row 9 K1, M1, k4, SKP, turn.
Rows 10, 12, 14, 16, and 18 With A, k1 (twisting with B yarn to prevent hole in work); with B, k to end of row.
Row 11 With B, k1, M1, k5, bring B to front of work; with A, SKP, turn.
Row 13 With B, k1, M1, k6, bring B to front of work; with A, SKP, turn.
Row 15 With B, k1, M1, k7, bring B to front of work; with A, SKP, turn.
Row 17 With B, k1, M1, k8, bring B to front of work; with A, SKP, turn.
Row 19 With B, k1, M1, k9, bring B to front of work; with A, SKP, turn.

MEASUREMENTS
BLANKET
34"/86.5cm square
SQUARE
4"/10cm cube

MATERIALS
- 3½oz/100g and 215yd/197m skein of any cotton/wool blend
- 4 skein each in Black (A) and White (A)
- One size 7 (4.5mm) circular needle, 32"/80cm long, or size to obtain gauge
- One pair size 6 (4mm) needles
- Stitch markers
- Optional: One 4"/10cm foam cube

GAUGE
19 sts and 37 rows to 4"/10cm over garter st using size 7 (4.5mm) needles.
TAKE TIME TO CHECK YOUR GAUGE.

STRIPE SEQUENCE
10 rows in A, 10 rows in B.
Rep these 20 rows for the stripe sequence.

NOTE
Circular needle is used to accommodate the large number of stitches of the blanket. Do *not* join.

Row 20 With A, k to end of row.
Cont as established, foll stripe sequence, keeping first st of RS row/last st of WS row in A, and on RS always working M1 after first st of every RS row and working 1 additional st before the SKP at end of every RS short row, until 115 sts rem on LH needle, end with a RS row.

DECREASING EDGE
Cont in stripe sequence, keeping first st of RS row/last st of WS row in A, work as foll:
Dec row (WS) SKP, k114, SKP, turn.
Next row and all RS rows K to end of row.
Dec row (WS) SKP, k113, SKP, turn.
Cont as now established, working 1 less st before the SKP, until 1 st rem on LH needle, end with a RS row.
Dec row (WS) [SKP] twice—2 sts.
Dec row K2tog. Fasten off.

Finishing
Weave in ends. Lightly block to measurements.

BLOCK
Square 1 (make 2)
With straight needles and A, cast on 1 st.
Inc row 1 (RS) Kfb—2 sts.
Inc row 2 Kfb, k1—3 sts.
Inc row 3 K1, M1, k to end of row—1 st inc'd.
Rep row 3 until there are 31 sts, end with a WS row.
Dec row (RS) SKP, k to end of row—1 st dec'd.
Rep last row until 2 sts rem.
Dec row K2tog. Fasten off.

Square 2 (make 2)
With B, work same as for square 1.

Square 3 (make 2)
With A, cast on 1 st.
Foll stripe sequence, work same as for square 1.

Finishing
Weave in ends.
Foll assembly diagram and with RS facing, sew squares tog to form a cube, leaving one side open. Insert foam cube and sew closed.

ASSEMBLY DIAGRAM

		SQUARE 2	
SQUARE 1	SQUARE 3	SQUARE 1	SQUARE 3
		SQUARE 2	

130

BONUS BLOCK
You should have enough yarn to make the blanket and toy block. If you don't want to buy a foam block, you could use polyester stuffing instead.

Stained Glass Blanket

DESIGNED BY Karen Baumers

Eighty-one garter-stitch squares in many two-color combinations are arranged to create a vivid stained-glass effect.

MEASUREMENTS
54"/137cm square

MATERIALS
- 3½oz/100g and 220yd/210m skein of any wool (4)
  2 skeins each in Red (A), Orange (B), Yellow (C), Gold (D), Aqua (E), Bright Blue (F), Lime Green (G), Green (H), Pink (J)
  1 skein in Dark Pink (I)
- One pair size 6 (4mm) needles, *or size to obtain gauge*

GAUGES
- 19 sts and 34 rows to 4"/10cm over garter st using size 6 (4mm) needles.
- Each square measures 6"/15cm square.

TAKE TIME TO CHECK YOUR GAUGES.

NOTES
1) Squares are worked diagonally, changing colors at widest point.
2) The color diagram shows the colors and placements of the squares as shown in the photo. To design your own colorway and placement of squares, use the blank grid provided to draw in your customized design.

SQUARE
With first color, cast on 2 sts.
Inc row 1 (RS) K1, kfb—3 sts.
Inc row 2 K1, kfb, k to end—1 st inc'd.
Rep row 2 for 36 times more—40 sts.
Change to 2nd color.
Dec row (RS) K1, k2tog—1 st dec'd.
Rep dec row 37 times more—2 sts rem.
Final row K2tog. Fasten off.

AFGHAN
Make 81 squares total in colors as foll:
- 1 each in A and I, D and G, E and I, F and G, G and I, H and I.
- 2 each in E and G, F and I.
- 3 each in E and H, F and J, G and J.
- 4 each in C and G, F and H, G and H, H and J.
- 5 each in A and C; A and D, B and C, C and D, I and J.
- 6 in E and F.
- 7 in B and D.
- 8 in A and B.

Finishing
Block squares to measurements.
Foll placement diagram, arrange in 9 rows of 9 squares each.
Seam squares together using mattress st over garter st (see page 181) into 9 strips of 9 squares each.
Seam strips tog. Weave in rem ends. ■

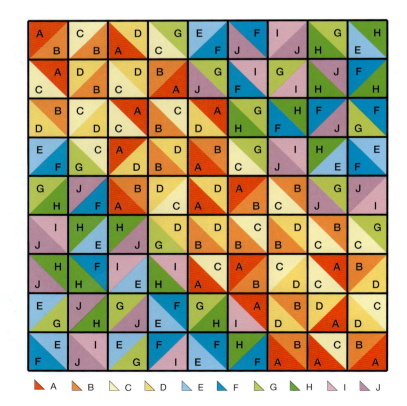

132

FRIENDS WITH THE ENDS
Leaving long tails on these squares will give you yarn that you can later use to seam them together.

Buddy Bunny Blanket

DESIGNED BY Katherine Mehls

Bunny motifs created with a bobble "tail" nestled among clever cables create a field of adorable fluffy friends. Squishy garter stitch borders make the perfect frame.

MEASUREMENTS
Width 30"/76cm
Length 36"/91.5cm

MATERIALS
- 1¾oz/50g and 125yd/112m skein of any cotton
- 9 skeins in Pink
- One size 6 (4mm) circular needle, 29"/74cm long, *or size to obtain gauge*
- Cable needle (cn)
- Stitch markers

GAUGE
22 sts and 34 rows to 4"/10cm over St st using size 6 (4mm) needle.
TAKE TIME TO CHECK YOUR GAUGE.

NOTE
Circular needle is used to accommodate the large number of stitches. Do not turn.

STITCH GLOSSARY
4-st RC Sl 2 sts to cn, hold to *back* of work, k2, k2 from cn.
4-st LC Sl 2 sts to cn, hold to *front* of work, k2, k2 from cn.
8-st RC Sl 4 sts to cn, hold to *back* of work, k4, k4 from cn.
MB (make bobble) ([K1, yo] twice, k1) into same st to inc to 5 sts, turn; p5, turn; k5, turn; p5, turn; ssk, k1, k2tog, turn; p3, turn; sl 1, k2tog, psso—bobble complete, 1 st rem.

BLANKET
Using long-tail cast-on, cast on 194 sts.
****Row 1 (WS)** *K38, pm, p1 (for St st); rep from * 3 times more, k38.
Row 2 (RS) Knit.
Rep rows 1 and 2 four times more for a total of 5 garter ridges.
Next row (WS) *K6, p7, k2, p8, k2, p7, k6, sm, p1; rep from * 3 times more, k6, p7, k2, p8, k2, p7, k6.

Bunny Pattern
Row 1 (RS) *K13, p2, 4-st RC, 4-st LC, p2, k13, sm, k1; rep from * 3 times more, k13, p2, 4-st RC, 4-st LC, p2, k13.
Row 2 *K6, p7, k2, p8, k2, p7, k6, sm, p1; rep from * 3 times more, k6, p7, k2, p8, k2, p7, k6.
Row 3 *K13, p2, k8, p2, k13, sm k1; rep from * 3 times more, k13, p2, k8, p2, k13.
Row 4 Rep row 2.

TAIL
Row 5 (RS) *K13, p2, k4, MB, k3, p2, k13, sm, k1; rep from * 3 times more, k13, p2, k4, MB, k3, p2, k13.
Rows 6–11 Rep rows 2 and 3 three times more.
Row 12 Rep row 2.

HEAD
Row 13 (RS) *K13, p2, 8-st RC, p2, k13, sm, k1; rep from * 3 times more, k13, p2, 8-st RC, p2, k13.
Rows 14–20 Rep rows 6–12.

EARS
Row 21 (RS) Rep row 13.
Row 22 *K6, p7, k2, p2, k4, p2, k2, p7, k6, sm, p1; rep from * 3 times more, k6, p7, k2, p2, k4, p2, k2, p7, k6.
Row 23 *K13, p2, k2, p4, k2, p2, k13, sm, k1; rep from * 3 times more, k13, p2, k2, p4, k2, p2, k13.
Rows 24–27 Rep rows 22 and 23 twice more.
Row 28 Rep row 22.
Row 29 *K13, cast on 1 st, p2, ssk, p4, k2tog, p2, cast on 1 st, k13, sm, k1; rep from * 3 times more, k13, cast on 1 st, p2, ssk, p4, k2tog, p2, cast on 1 st, k13.

Garter Border
Row 1 (WS) *K to marker, sm, p1; rep from * 3 times more, k to end.
Row 2 Knit.
Rep Rows 1 and 2 four times more for a total of 5 garter ridges.++

Block Divider
Row 1 (WS) Purl.
Row 2 Knit.
Rep rows 1 and 2 three times more.**

Rep from ** to ** 4 times more.
Rep from ** to ++ once more, end at completion of a garter border.
Bind off.

Finishing
Weave in ends. Block to measurements.

COLOR CHANGE
This blanket looks incredible in a single color, but consider knitting each row of blocks in a different color. Try blues or pinks or a range of pastels or even rainbow colors.

Stronger Together Blanket

DESIGNED BY Katharine Hunt

Three panels of smocking stitch and simple ribbing combine for maximum coziness. An invisible weaving technique joins everything together beautifully.

MEASUREMENTS
Width 49"/124.5cm
Length (without fringe) 55"/140cm

MATERIALS
- 3½oz/100g and 110yd/101m skein of any wool (5)
- 18 skeins in White
- One pair size 15 (10mm) needles, *or size to obtain gauge*
- One size N/P-15 (10mm) crochet hook
- Stitch markers

GAUGE
13¼ sts and 14 rows to 4"/10cm over smocking st using size 15 (10mm) needles.
TAKE TIME TO CHECK YOUR GAUGE.

NOTE
Blanket is knit in three separate panels, two side panels and one center panel, then sewn tog.

SMOCKING STITCH
(multiple of 8 sts plus 2)
Row 1 (RS) P2, *k2, p2; rep from * to end.
Row 2 and all WS rows K2, *p2, k2; rep from * to end.
Row 3 P2, *bring yarn to back, insert RH needle from front between 6th and 7th sts on LH needle and draw through a lp; sl this lp onto LH needle and k it tog with first st on LH needle; k1, p2, k2, p2; rep from * to end.
Row 5 Rep row 1.
Row 7 P2, k2, p2, *bring yarn to back, draw lp as before and k it tog with first st on LH needle; then k1, p2, k2, p2; rep from * to last 4 sts, k2, p2.
Row 8 K2, *p2, k2; rep from * to end.
Rep rows 1–8 for smocking st.

INVISIBLE SEAM
Place pieces to be joined on a flat surface with RS facing.
Begin atz lower edge, insert tapestry needle under bottom lp of a purl st on one side of seam, and then under a top lp of corresponding purl st on opposite side. Pull yarn through, tightening seam just enough to merge two pieces.
Cont to alternate from side to side in every st.

BLANKET
Side Panels (make 2)
Cast on 50 sts.
Row 1 (RS) P2, *k2, p2; rep from * to end.
Row and all WS rows K2, *p2, k2; rep from * to end.
Rep last 2 rows for k2, p2 rib twice more.

SMOCKING STITCH
Next row (RS) Rib 12 sts as established, pm, work row 1 of smocking st over next 26 sts, pm, rib 12 sts as established.
Next row Rib 12, sm, work next row of smocking st over next 26 sts, sm, rib 12. Cont in pats as established until rows 1–8 of smocking st have been worked 22 times, then work rows 1–4 once more. Remove markers and cont rib over all sts for 6 rows. Bind off in rib.
Rep for 2nd side panel.

Center Panel
Cast on 66 sts.
Work in k2, p2 rib same as for side panels for 6 rows.

SMOCKING STITCH
Work in smocking st over all sts until rows 1–8 of smocking st have been worked 22 times, then work rows 1–4 once more.
Cont rib over all sts for 6 rows.
Bind off in rib.

Finishing
Weave in ends. Block each panel lightly. Using invisible seam, sew panels tog with a side panel on each side of center panel.

FRINGE
Cut 240 strands of yarn, each 16"/40.5cm long.
Hold 3 strands tog and fold in half. With RS of blanket facing, insert hook through center of k2 rib from back to front, hook middle of strands, and pull strands through to form a lp. Bring lp around edge

FIND YOUR FRINGE

This pattern describes a specific way to add the fringe, but you can experiment with the fringe length, number of strands held together, and frequency along the edges to find your ideal ratio.

of blanket to front, thread tails through lp, tighten lp to secure fringe.
Rep in each k2 rib along cast-on and bound-off edges. Trim fringe as needed.

Gridded Blanket

DESIGNED BY Sandi Prosser

Bands of seed stitch block off stockinette stitch into a graphic grid pattern that is as easy to knit as it is satisfying.

MEASUREMENTS
Width 49"/124.5cm
Length 53"/134.5cm

MATERIALS
- 3½oz/100g and 108yd/100m skein of any alpaca (5)
- 16 skeins in Gray
- One size 10 (6mm) circular needle, 32"/80cm long, *or size to obtain gauge*

GAUGE
16 sts and 22 rows to 4"/10cm over textured st pat using size 10 (6mm) needle.
TAKE TIME TO CHECK YOUR GAUGE.

NOTES
1) Circular needle is used to accommodate the large number of stitches. Do not join.
2) To make your gauge swatch, cast on a multiple of 10 stitches plus 3 more, and then repeat rows 1-10 of the textured stitch pattern.

SEED STITCH
(odd number of sts)
Row 1 (RS) K1, *p1, k1; rep from * to end.
Row 2 P the knit sts and k the purl sts.
Rep row 2 for seed st.

BLANKET
Cast on 193 sts.
Work 11 rows in seed st, end with a WS row.

Textured Stitch Pattern
Rows 1, 3, 5, and 7 (RS) K1, *p1, k9; rep from * to last 2 sts, p1, k1.
Rows 2, 4, 6, and 8 *K1, p1, k1, p7; rep from * to last 3 sts, k1, p1, k1.
Row 9 *[K1, p1] 21 times, k8; rep from * twice more, [k1, p1] 21 times, k1.
Row 10 *[K1, p1] 21 times, k1, p7; rep from * twice more, [k1, p1] 21 times, k1.
Rep rows 1-10 five times more.
Rows 61, 63, 65, and 67 (RS) K1, p1, k to last 2 sts, p1, k1.
Rows 62, 64, 66, and 68 K1, p1, k1, p to last 3 sts, k1, p1, k1.
Rows 69 and 70 Rep rows 9 and 10.
Rep rows 1-70 for textured st pat twice, then rep rows 1-58 once more.
Work 11 rows in seed st, end with a RS row. Bind off in pat.

Finishing
Weave in ends. Block lightly to measurements.

THE INCREDIBLE BULK
Thicker yarns make larger stitches, meaning fewer stitches will take up more space than the same number of stitches in a finer yarn. Projects with heavier yarns whip up faster, which is great if you're in a rush to complete a project.

Chevron Pop Blanket

DESIGNED BY The Knit Simple Design Team

A classic chevron pattern is electrified with neon colors and garter ridge stripes.

MEASUREMENTS
35½ x 40"/90 x 101.5cm

MATERIALS
- 4oz/113g and 203yd/186m skein of any acrylic
- 4 skeins in Bright Violet (A)
- 1 skein each in Neon Orange (B) and Neon Pink (C)
- One size 9 (5.5mm) circular needle, 32"/80cm long, *or size to obtain gauge*

GAUGE
19 sts and 24 rows to 4"/10cm over welted chevron pat using size 9 (5.5mm) needles.
TAKE TIME TO CHECK YOUR GAUGE.

NOTES
1) Circular needle is used to accommodate the large number of stitches. Do not join.
2) To make your gauge swatch, cast on a multiple of 11 stitches plus 14 more, and then repeat rows 1-12 of the welted chevron pattern. You may knit the gauge swatch in one color only.

AFGHAN
With A, cast on 168 sts. Work rows 5 rows in garter st (k every row).

Welted Chevron Pattern
Rows 1, 3, 5, and 7 (RS) With A, k7, *k2tog, k2, [kfb] twice, k3, ssk; rep from * to last 7 sts, k7.
Rows 2, 4, and 6 With A, k7, p to last 7 sts, k7.
Row 8 With A, knit.
Rows 9-12 With B or C, knit.
Rep rows 1-12 for welted chevron pat, alternating B and C for rows 9-12, until piece measures 38"/96.5cm from beg, end with a pat row 12.
With A only, work rows 1-12 once more. Bind off.

Finishing
Weave in ends. Block to measurements.

CARRY OR CUT?
When leaving a color on hold for only a few rows, as with color A here, you may carry it along the side until it's needed again, instead of cutting it and rejoining it later.

Purl Stitch Snowflake Blanket

DESIGNED BY Rosemary Drysdale

Horizontal and vertical bands of garter stitch form a checkerboard of Stockinette stitch and knit/purl snowflake motifs.

MEASUREMENTS
Width 29"/73.5cm
Length 23"/58.5cm

MATERIALS
- 3½oz/100g and 218yd/196m skein of any superwash wool (4)
- 3 hanks in White
- One pair size 7 (4.5mm) needles, *or size to obtain gauge*
- Stitch markers

GAUGE
20 sts and 24 rows to 4"/10cm over St st using size 7 (4.5mm) needles.
TAKE TIME TO CHECK YOUR GAUGE.

BLANKET
Cast on 147 sts.
Work in garter st (k every row) for 8 rows.

Block Pat
TIER 1
Row 1 (RS) K6 (garter st border), pm, [work row 1 of snowflake chart over 23 sts, pm, k5 (garter st band), pm, k23 (St st square), pm, k5 (garter st band), pm] twice, work row 1 of snowflake chart over 23 sts, pm, k6 (garter st border).
Row 2 K6, sm, [work row 2 of snowflake chart over 23 sts, sm, k5, sm, p23, sm, k5, sm] twice, work row 2 of snowflake chart over 23 sts, sm, k6.
Cont in pats as established for 20 rows more.
Knit 8 rows.

TIER 2
Row 1 (RS) K6, sm, [k23 (St st square), sm, k5, work row 1 of snowflake chart over 23 sts, sm, k5, sm] twice, k23, sm, k6.
Cont in pats as established for 21 rows more.
Knit 8 rows.

Rep tier 1 and then tier 2 once more.
Rep tier 1 once more.
Knit 8 rows. Bind off knitwise.

FINISHING
Weave in ends. Block to measurements. ■

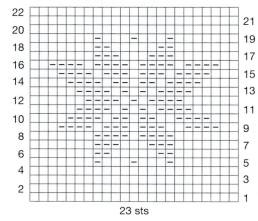

SNOWFLAKE CHART

STITCH KEY
☐ k on RS, p on WS
⊟ p on RS, k on WS

MORE OR LESS
Adapt this blanket by working the snowflake motif and Stockinette squares in whichever layout and ratio you prefer.

Turtle Lace Blanket

DESIGNED BY Lisa Craig

An easy lace pattern reminiscent of little turtles looks all the more beautiful when knit in a soft chunky-weight alpaca yarn. Garter stitch borders are worked in simultaneously.

MEASUREMENTS
Width 36"/90cm
Length 49"/124cm

MATERIALS
- 3½oz/100g and 110yd/100m skein of any baby alpaca (5)
- 9 skeins in Sea Green
- One pair each size 10 and 10½ (6 and 6.5mm) needles, *or size to obtain gauge*

GAUGE
12 sts and 18 rows to 4"/10cm over lace pat using larger needles.
TAKE TIME TO CHECK YOUR GAUGE.

LACE PATTERN
(begins with a multiple of 6 sts plus 9)
Note Stitch rep alternates between 6 sts and 8 sts.
Row 1 (RS) K4, *k1, yo, SKP, k1, k2tog, yo; rep from * to last 5 sts, k5.
Row 2 and all WS rows K3, p to last 3 sts, k3.
Row 3 K4, *k2, yo, k3, yo, k1; rep from * to last 5 sts, k5.
Row 5 K4, k2tog, *yo, SKP, k1, k2tog, yo, SK2P; rep from * to last 11 sts, yo, SKP, k1, k2tog, yo, SKP, k4.
Row 7 K4, *k1, k2tog, yo, k1, yo, SKP, rep from * to last 5 sts, K5.
Row 9 Rep row 3.
Row 11 K4, *k1, k2tog, yo, SK2P, yo, SKP, rep from * to last 5 sts, k5.
Row 12 K3, p to last 3 sts, k3.
Rep rows 1–12 for lace pat.

BLANKET
With smaller needles, cast on 111 sts.
Work 10 rows of garter st (k every row).
Change to larger needles.
Rep rows 1–12 of lace pat until blanket measures approx 47"/120cm, end with a pat row 12.
Change to smaller needles.
Work 10 rows of garter st. Bind off.

Finishing
Weave in ends. Block to measurements.

OPENING UP
Lace patterns often scrunch up until they are blocked. Blocking a lace pattern relaxes the fibers and helps the stitches settle so the lace pattern can shine.

Garden Patch Lapghan

KNITTED BY Nicole Milano

A checkerboard of stockinette and seed stitch squares, all knit in one piece and framed with garter stitch, makes a textural and cozy delight.

MEASUREMENTS
Width 30"/76cm
Length 41"/104cm

MATERIALS
- 3½oz/100g and 52yd/48m skein of any wool
- 9 skeins in Pink
- One pair size 13 (9mm) needles, *or size to obtain gauges*
- Stitch markers

GAUGES
- 10 sts and 13 rows to 4"/10cm over St st using size 13 (9mm) needles.
- 9 sts and 12 rows to 4"/10cm over seed st using size 13 (9mm) needles.

TAKE TIME TO CHECK YOUR GAUGES.

BLOCK PATTERN
(multiple of 18 sts plus 9)
Note Block pat can be worked from written instructions or chart.
Row 1 (RS) K9, *[p1, k1] 4 times, p1; rep from * to end.
Row 2 *P10, [k1, p1] 4 times; rep from * to last 9 sts, p9.
Rows 3–12 Rep rows 1 and 2 five times more.
Row 13 [P1, k1] 4 times, p1, *k9, [p1, k1] 4 times, p1; rep from * to end.
Row 14 *[P1, k1] 4 times, p10; rep from * to last 9 sts, [p1, k1] 4 times, p1.
Rows 15–24 Rep rows 13 and 14 five times more.
Rep rows 1–24 for block pat.

LAPGHAN
Cast on 69 sts.
Beg with a WS row, knit 3 rows.

Block Pattern
Row 1 (RS) K3 (garter st border), pm, work block pat to last 3 sts, pm, k3 (garter st border).
Row 2 K3, sm, work next row of block pat to marker, sm, k3.
Cont in pats as established, keeping first and last 3 sts in garter st (k every row), until 24 rows of block pat have been worked 6 times.
Knit 3 rows over all sts.
Bind off knitwise on WS.

Finishing
Weave in ends. Block to measurements.

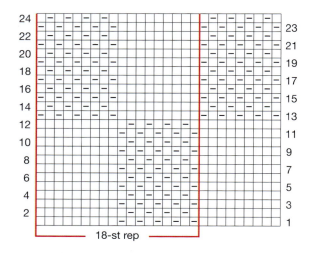

STITCH KEY
☐ k on RS, p on WS
⊟ p on RS, k on WS

CUSTOM SIZES
For simple patterns with simple repeats, like this blanket, adjust the final size by adding or removing stitch repeats (here, it is 18 stitches) and row repeats (here, it is 24 rows). Just make sure to buy plenty of yarn if going larger!

Garter Gingham Blanket

DESIGNED BY Audrey Drysdale

Holding two strands together makes this blanket twice as fast to knit. Knit seven strips, seam them together, weave in your ends, and then enjoy this comfy blanket.

MEASUREMENTS
Width 46"/117cm
Length 60"/152.5cm

MATERIALS
- 1¾oz/50g and 114yd/104m skein of any wool
- 24 skeins in Light Gray (A)
- 18 skeins in Dark Gray (B)
- 8 skeins in Cream (C)
- One pair size 10½ (6.5mm) needles, or size to obtain gauge

GAUGE
15½ sts and 26 rows to 4"/10cm over garter st using size 10½ (6.5mm) needles and 2 strands of yarn held tog. *TAKE TIME TO CHECK YOUR GAUGE.*

NOTES
1) Blanket is made in 7 separate strips, then sewn together.
2) Hold 2 strands of yarn together throughout, even when seaming.

BLANKET

Strip 1 (make 4)
With 2 strands of B held tog, cast on 25 sts.
Row 1 (WS) Knit.
Cont in garter st (k every row) for 40 rows more.
*Cut B strands, join 2 strands of A.
Knit 42 rows.
Cut A strands, join 2 strands of B.
Knit 42 rows.*
Rep between *s 3 times more. Bind off.

Strip 2 (make 3)
With 2 strands of A held tog, cast on 25 sts.
Row 1 (WS) Knit.
Cont in garter st for 40 rows more.
*Cut A strands, join 2 strands of C.
Knit 42 rows.
Cut C strands, join 2 strands of A.
Knit 42 rows.*
Rep between *s 3 times more. Bind off.

Finishing
Weave in ends. Block lightly.
Arrange strips, alternating strips 1 and 2, with strip 1 on each outside edge.
Using mattress st over garter st (see page 181), sew strips tog.

MARL MAGIC
Knitting with multiple strands of different colors of yarn held together is called marling. The yarns naturally twist around each other as you knit, creating beautiful depth of color.

Candy Cabin Afghan & Pillow

DESIGNED BY Beth Whiteside

Start with a bright center in a single color before moving on to the color-shifting edges of these log cabin squares.

MEASUREMENTS

Afghan
Width 47"/119.5cm
Length 57"/145cm
Pillow 18"/46cm square

MATERIALS

- 3½oz/100g and 150yd/138m skein of any wool (4)
- 17 skeins (for afghan) and 2 skeins (for front of pillow) in self-striping colors (A)
- 1 skein each in Blue (B), Purple (C), Green (D), Aqua (E), and Coral (F)
- One pair size 9 (5.5mm) needles, *or size to obtain gauges*
- One extra size 9 (5.5mm) needle
- Two size 9 (5.5mm) circular needles, 40"/100cm long
- 18"/45cm square pillow form
- 18"/45cm square piece of felt in coordinating color

GAUGES

- 17 sts and 36 rows to 4"/10cm over garter st using size 9 (5.5 mm) needles.
- One block to approx 9"/23cm square using size 9 (5.5 mm) needles.

TAKE TIME TO CHECK YOUR GAUGES.

NOTES

1) Blocks are worked in a tier of logs around a center square. The cast-on row counts as the first right-side row.
2) When picking up stitches, pick up one stitch for every garter stitch ridge (two rows).
3) The last stitch of the previous square or log becomes the first stitch of the next log, and counts as the stitch of the first ridge.
4) Weave in ends as you go to minimize finishing.
5) Circular needle is used to accommodate the large number of stitches. Do not turn.

AFGHAN

Log Cabin Block
Make 6 blocks each with B, C, D, E, and F for center square—30 blocks total.

CENTER BLOCK
With B, C, D, E, or F, cast on 13 sts.
Knit 25 rows, end with a WS row. Bind off to last st, leave last st on needle. Cut yarn.
With RS facing, rotate block clockwise 90 degrees.

LOG 1
Join A. Pick up and k 12 sts along side of center square—13 sts.
Knit 25 rows, end with a WS row. Bind off to last st, leaving it on the needle.
With RS facing, rotate work clockwise 90 degrees.

LOG 2
Pick up and k 12 sts along side of log 1 and 13 sts along cast-on edge of center square—26 sts.
Knit 25 rows, end with a WS row. Bind off to last st, leaving it on the needle.
With RS facing, rotate work clockwise 90 degrees.

LOG 3
Pick up and k 12 sts along side of log 2 and 13 sts along side of center square—26 sts.
Knit 25 rows, end with a WS row. Bind off to last st, leaving it on the needle.
With RS facing, rotate work clockwise 90 degrees.

LOG 4
Pick up and k 12 sts along side of log 3, 13 sts along bound-off edge of center square, and 13 sts along side edge of log 1—39 sts.
Knit 25 rows, end with a WS row. Bind off.

Weave in ends. Block the 30 log cabin blocks.

Strips
Referring to diagram for placement, arrange blocks in five vertical strips of six blocks each.

VERTICAL STRIPS
With A and RS facing, pick up and k 39 sts along top edge of one block and the bottom edge of an adjacent block, leaving yarn attached to one.
Holding needles parallel with WS of blocks held tog, use extra needle to join using 3-needle bind-off to join.
Rep for each block in the vertical strip. Then rep for each vertical strip.

JOIN VERTICAL STRIPS
With RS facing, circular needle and A, pick up and k 39 sts along each block and 2

LOG CABIN FEVER

Log cabin knitting begins with a small section and grows larger by picking up stitches to knit new sections from what was previously knitted. Garter stitch's texture and gauge keep log cabin knitting tidy and simple.

sts along join between blocks along right edge of one strip—244 sts. Cut A.
Rep pick up along left edge of adjacent strip, leaving yarn attached.
Holding needles parallel with WS of strips held tog, use extra needle and join using 3-needle bind-off (see page 173).
Repeat for all strips.

Borders

Note The stitch left on the needle before rotating work 90 degrees does not contribute to block pick-up stitch counts.

BORDER TIER 1
With RS facing and B, beg at top left corner of afghan, pick up and k 39 sts per block along side edge and 2 sts between blocks—244 sts.
Knit 1 row. Bind off to last st, leaving it on needle.
With RS facing, rotate work 90 degrees.

Pick up and k 39 sts per block and 2 sts between blocks along bottom of afghan—204 sts.
Knit 1 row. Bind off to last st, leaving it on needle.
With RS facing, rotate work 90 degrees.

Pick up and k 39 sts per block and 2 sts between blocks along side of afghan—245 sts.
Knit 1 row. Bind off to last st, leaving it on needle.
With RS facing, rotate work 90 degrees.

Pick up and k 39 sts per block, 2 sts between blocks, and 1 st per ridge of border along top of afghan—205 sts.
Knit 1 row. Bind off to last st, leaving it on needle.
With RS facing, rotate work 90 degrees. Cut yarn.

BORDER TIER 2
Join F.
Pick up and k 1 st in each st and 1 st in ridge of left side border—246 sts.
Knit 1 row. Bind off to last st, leaving it on needle.
With RS facing, rotate work 90 degrees.

Pick up and k 1 st in each st and 1 st in each ridge of bottom border—206 sts.
Knit 1 row. Bind off to last st, leaving it on needle.
With RS facing, rotate work 90 degrees.

Pick up and k 1 st in each st and 1 st in each ridge of right side border—247 sts.
Knit 1 row. Bind off to last st, leaving it on needle.
With RS facing, rotate work 90 degrees.

Pick up and k 1 st in each st and 1 st in each ridge of top border—207 sts.
Knit 1 row. Bind off to last st, leaving it on needle.
With RS facing, rotate work 90 degrees. Cut yarn.

BORDER TIER 3
Join E.
Work same as for border tier 2, picking up 1 st in each st and 1 st in each ridge of border; stitch counts increase by two sts each log. Cut yarn.

Finishing
Weave in ends. Block to measurements.

PILLOW
Log Cabin Block
Note Pillow in photo was made with a felt backing. If desired, a 2nd set of blocks can be knit for the back.
Make four blocks with desired color(s) for center squares.
Join squares using 3-needle bind-off same as for afghan.
Sew 18"/46cm square felt piece to knitted piece, leaving one side open.
Insert pillow form and sew rem side.

AFGHAN ASSEMBLY DIAGRAM

BLOCK DIAGRAM

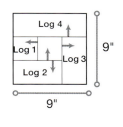

Direction of work

845 denim (B)   249 amethyst (C) 240 jasmine green (D) 849 dark aqua (E) 242 deep coral (F)

153

Shifting Chevron Blanket

DESIGNED BY Sandi Prosser

The depth of this chevron's stripes changes across the color sequence, causing additional waves. A bonus block in the same tones makes a perfect surprise add-on.

MEASUREMENTS
Blanket
Width 27"/68.5cm
Length 30"/76cm
Block 4"/10cm cube

MATERIALS
- 3oz/85g and 197yd/180m skein of any acrylic/wool blend (4)
- 2 skeins each in Purple (A), Medium Purple (B), and Light Pink (C)
- One size 8 (5mm) circular needle, 32"/80cm long, *or size to obtain gauge*
- One pair size 7 (4.5mm) needles
- Removable stitch markers
- One 4"/10cm foam cube

GAUGE
22 sts and 23 rows to 4"/10cm over chevron pat using size 8 (5mm) needle.
TAKE TIME TO CHECK YOUR GAUGE.

NOTES
1) Circular needle is used to accommodate the large number of stitches. Do *not* join.
2) When changing colors at beg of RS rows, sl 1 wyif, k2 and then join new color.

CHEVRON PATTERN
(multiple of 24 sts plus 25 plus 6 edge sts)
Row 1 (RS) Sl 1 wyif, k2, k2tog, k10, *M1R, k1, M1L, k10, S2KP, k10; rep from * to last 16 sts, M1R, k1, M1L, k10, ssk, k3.
Row 2 Sl 1 wyif, k to end.
Row 3 Sl 1 wyif, k2, k2tog, k10, *M1R, k1, M1L, k10, S2KP, k10; rep from * to last 16 sts, M1R, k1, M1L, k10, ssk, k3.
Row 4 Sl 1 wyif, k2, p to last 2 sts, k3.
Rep rows 3 and 4 for chevron pat.

STRIPE SEQUENCE
Work 16 rows with A; 10 rows with B; 16 rows with C;
16 rows with B; 16 rows with A; 10 rows with C;
16 rows with B; 16 rows with C; 16 rows with A;
10 rows with C; 16 rows with A; 13 rows with B.

BLANKET
With circular needle and A, cast on 151 sts.
Knit 1 row on WS.
Work in chevron pat and stripe sequence to end of stripe sequence (171 rows).
Next row (WS) With B, sl 1 wyif, k to end.
Next row (RS) With B, work row 1 of chevron pat.
Bind off all sts knitwise.

FINISHING
Weave in ends. Lightly block to measurements.

BLOCK
Side Panel
With size 7 (4.5mm) needles and A, cast on 20 sts.
Beg with a knit (RS) row, work in St st (k on RS, p on WS) for 2"/5cm, end with a RS row.
Next row (WS) Knit, pm at each end of row.
Cut A, join C.
With C, cont in St st for 4"/10cm, end with a RS row.
Next row (WS) Knit, pm at each end of row.
Cut C, join A.
With A, cont in St st for 4"/10cm, end with a RS row.
Next row (WS) Knit, pm at each end of row.
Cut A, join B.
With B, cont in St st for 4"/10cm, end with a RS row.
Next row (WS) Knit, pm at each end of row.
Cut B, join A.

BONUS BLOCK
You should have enough yarn to make the blanket and toy block. If you don't want to buy a foam block, you could use polyester stuffing instead.

With A, cont in St st for 2"/5cm, end with a WS row.
Bind off.

Top
With size 7 (4.5mm) needles and C, cast on 20 sts.
Beg with a knit (RS) row, work in St st for 4"/10cm, end with a WS row. Bind off.

Base
With size 7 (4.5mm) needles and B, cast on 20 sts.
Beg with a knit (RS) row, work in St st for 4"/10cm, end with a WS row. Bind off.

Finishing
Weave in ends.
Sew cast-on edge of side panel to bound-off edge.
Sew top and bottom to side panel, matching corners of top and bottom to markers of side panel, leaving one side edge open.
Insert foam cube and sew rem side edge.

Garter Stitch Basket

DESIGNED BY Matthew Schrank

This beautiful basket starts with a Stockinette stitch base worked in the round to the desired circumference. The garter stitch sides are then worked in the round.

MEASUREMENTS
Circumference 26½"/67cm
Height 9"/23cm

MATERIALS
- 7oz/200g and 110yd/100m skein of any acrylic/wool/nylon blend
- 2 skeins in Coral
- One size 13 (9mm) circular needle, 24"/60cm long, *or size to obtain gauge*
- One set (4) size 13 (9mm) double-pointed needles (dpn)
- Stitch marker

GAUGE
9 sts and 20 rnds to 4"/10cm over garter st using size 13 (9mm) needle.
TAKE TIME TO CHECK YOUR GAUGE.

BASKET
Note Change to circular needle when sts no longer fit comfortably on dpn.
With dpn, cast on 6 sts and divide sts evenly over 3 needles. Join, take care not to twist sts, and pm for beg of rnd.
Inc rnd 1 Kfb in each st—12 sts.
Rnd 2 and all even rnds through rnd 18 Knit.
Inc rnd 3 [Kfb, k1] 6 times—18 sts.
Inc rnd 5 [Kfb, k2] 6 times—24 sts.
Inc rnd 7 [Kfb, k3] 6 times—30 sts.
Inc rnd 9 [Kfb, k4] 6 times—36 sts.
Inc rnd 11 [Kfb, k5] 6 times—42 sts.
Inc rnd 13 [Kfb, k6] 6 times—48 sts.
Inc rnd 15 [Kfb, k7] 6 times—54 sts.
Inc rnd 17 [Kfb, k8] 6 times—60 sts.
Rnd 19 Knit.
Rnd 20 Purl.
Rep last 2 rnds for garter st until garter st section measures 9"/23cm. Bind off.

Finishing.
Weave in ends.
If desired, cut a piece of heavy cardboard to fit circumference of base and place inside basket to help St st base lie flat.

MAKE A SET
Make a set of baskets of varying sizes. Simply change how many stitches are in the base before working the sides.

Textured Washcloths

DESIGNED BY Carla Scott and Rosemary Drysdale

Hand-stitched cotton washcloths are luxurious and super-fast to knit, so turn out a rainbow's worth to indulge yourself and your houseguests.

MEASUREMENTS
Approx 11"/28cm square

MATERIALS
- 3½oz/100g and 180yd/165m skein of any cotton (4)
- 1 skein each in Aqua, Turquoise, Peach, Yellow, and Green
- One pair size 10½ (6.5mm) needles, *or size to obtain gauge*

GAUGE
12 sts and 16 rows to 4"/10cm over St st and 2 strands of yarn held tog using size 10½ (6.5mm) needles.
TAKE TIME TO CHECK YOUR GAUGE.

MISTAKE RIB WASHCLOTH
Note Shown in aqua.
Cast on 35 sts.
Row 1 (RS) K3, *p1, k3; rep from * to end.
Row 2 K1, *p1, k3; rep from* to last 2 sts, p1, k1.
Rep rows 1 and 2 until piece measures approx 11"/28cm from beg, end with a RS row.
Bind off knitwise on WS.

Finishing
Weave in ends.

Woven Slip Stitch
Note Shown in turquoise.
Cast on 32 sts.
Row 1 (RS) K1, *bring yarn between needles to front, sl 1 wyif, bring yarn between needles to back, k1; rep from * to last st, k1.
Row 2 K1, p to last st, k1.
Row 3 K1, *k1, bring yarn between needles to front, sl 1 wyif, bring yarn between needles to back; rep from * to last st, k1.
Row 4 K1, p to last st, k1.
Rep rows 1–4 until piece measures approx 11"/28cm from beg, end with a RS row.
Bind off knitwise on WS.

Finishing
Weave in ends.

BASKETWEAVE WASHCLOTH
Note Shown in peach.
Cast on 33 sts.
Row 1 (RS) K3, *p3, k3; rep from * to end.
Row 2 P3, *k3, p3; rep from * to end.
Rows 3 and 4 K3, *p3, k3; rep from* to end.
Row 5 P3, *k3, p3; rep from * to end.
Row 6 K3, *p3, k3; rep from * to end.
Rep rows 1–6 for basketweave pat until piece measures approx 11"/28cm from beg, end with a pat row 6. Bind off knitwise on RS.

Finishing
Weave in ends.

SLIP-STITCH RIB WASHCLOTH
Note RS shown in yellow. WS shown in green.
Cast on 33 sts.
Row 1 (WS) K1, *p1, k1; rep from * to end.
Row 2 (RS) P1, *sl 1 wyif, p1; rep from * to end.
Rep rows 1 and 2 until piece measures approx 11"/28cm from beg, end with a RS row. Bind off knitwise on WS.

Finishing
Weave in ends.

GOTTA BE COTTON
For washcloths, make sure to use a cotton yarn that is absorbent and colorfast.

Potted Plant Cozies

DESIGNED BY Audrey Drysdale

Make sure you plants feel right at home with this duo of cute cozies. Worked in the round from the top down, a decrease round at the lower edge creates the tapered shape.

MEASUREMENTS
Circumference 16½"/42cm
Length 5½"/14cm

MATERIALS
- 3½oz/100g and 109yd/100m skein of any acrylic (5)
- 3 skeins in White
- One size 10½ (6.5mm) circular needle, 16"/40cm long, *or size to obtain gauge*
- Cable needle (cn)
- Stitch marker

GAUGE
13 sts and 17 rows to 4"/10cm over garter st using size 10½ (6.5mm) needle.
TAKE TIME TO CHECK YOUR GAUGE.

STITCH GLOSSARY
4-st LC Sl 1 st to cn and hold to front, k3, k1 from cn.

NOTES
1) Cozies will fit pots 6"/15cm in diameter and 5"/14cm deep.
2) 1 skein will make 1 cozy.

BOX STITCH COZY
Cast on 54 sts. Join, taking care not to twist sts, and pm for beg of rnd.
[Knit 1 rnd, purl 1 rnd] 5 times for garter st border.

Box Stitch
Rnds 1 and 2 *P2, k1; rep from * around.
Rnds 3 and 4 Knit.
Rep rnds 1–4 for box stitch until piece measures approx 4½"/11.5cm from beg, end with a rnd 2.

Dec rnd *K2tog, k4; rep from * around—45 sts.
Next rnd Knit.
Next 2 rnds *P1, k1, p2, k1; rep from * around.
Next 2 rnds Knit.
Next 2 rnds *P1, k1, p2, k1; rep from * around.
Bind off knitwise.

Finishing.
Weave in ends.

CABLE COZY
Cast on 54 sts. Join, taking care not to twist sts, and pm for beg of rnd.
[Knit 1 rnd, purl 1 rnd] 4 times for garter st border. Knit 1 rnd.
Inc rnd *P8, pfb; rep from * around—60 sts.

Cable Pattern
Rnd 1 *4-st LC, p2; rep from * around.
Rnd 2 *K4, p2; rep from * around.
Rnd 3 *K4, p2tog, yo; rep from * around.
Rnd 4 Rep rnd 2.
Rnd 5 *K4, yo, p2tog; rep from * around.
Rnd 6 Rep rnd 2.
Rep rnds 1–6 once, then rep rnds 1–3 once more.

Dec rnd *K1, k2tog, k1, p2; rep from * around—50 sts.
Next rnd *K3, yo, p2tog; rep from * around.
Next 2 rnds *K3, p2; rep from * around.
Bind off in pat.

Finishing
Weave in ends.

IT'S A CINCH
If the cozy's a little too big, weave strands of yarn through the top and bottom edges, put the cozy on the pot, then tighten and knot the strands to hold the cozy in place.

On the Market

DESIGNED BY Susan B. Anderson

This totable market bag in a cotton/linen blend is stitched from the base up in openwork bands, then divided for the garter-stitched handles.

MEASUREMENTS
Length (excluding handles)
16"/40.5cm
Circumference 25"/63.5cm

MATERIALS
- 1¾oz/50g and 105yd/96m skein of any cotton/linen blend (4)
- 4 skeins in green
- One size 7 (4.5mm) circular needle, *or size to obtain gauge*
- One set (4) size 7 (4.5mm) double-pointed needles (dpn)
- Stitch markers
- Stitch holders

GAUGE
20 sts and 30 rnds to 4"/10cm over pat st using size 7 (4.5mm) needle.
TAKE TIME TO CHECK YOUR GAUGE.

PATTERN STITCH
(multiple of 5 sts)
Rnds 1-3 *K4, p1; rep from * around.
Rnd 4 *Yo, k2tog, yo, k2tog, p1; rep from * around.
Rnds 5-12 Rep rnds 1-4 twice more.
Rnds 13-20 *K4, p1; rep from * around.
Rep rnds 1-20 for pat st.

BAG
Note Change to circular needle when sts no longer fit comfortably on dpn.
With dpn, cast on 9 sts and divide evenly over 3 needles. Join, taking care not to twist sts, and pm for beg of rnd.
Rnd 1 Knit.
Inc rnd 2 *Kfb; rep from * around—18 sts.
Rnd 3 Knit.
Inc rnd 4 *Kfb; rep from * around—36 sts.
Rnds 5 and 6 Knit.
Inc rnd 7 *K2, kfb; rep from * around—48 sts.
Rnd 8 Knit.
Inc rnd 9 *K3, kfb; rep from * around—60 sts.
Rnd 10 Knit.
Inc rnd 11 *K4, kfb; rep from * around—72 sts.
Rnds 12 and 13 Knit.
Inc rnd 14 *K5, kfb; rep from * around—84 sts.
Rnd 15 Knit.
Inc rnd 16 *K6, kfb; rep from * around—96 sts.
Inc rnd 17 *K23, kfb; rep from * around—100 sts.
Rnd 18 Knit.
Rnd 19 *K4, kfb; rep from * around—120 sts.
Rnds 20 and 21 Knit.
Rnd 22 *K11, kfb; rep from * around—130 sts. Place a 2nd marker in last st of rnd and do *not* slip this marker.

Pattern Stitch
Work rnds 1-20 of pat st 4 times, piece measures 10½"/26.5cm from marker.

Garter Border
[Knit 1 rnd, purl 1 rnd] 4 times.

Divide for Handles
Next rnd K65 sts, place rem 65 sts on holder for back.

Front Handle
Working first 65 sts only, turn and work as foll:
Dec row K1, ssk, k to last 3 sts, k2tog, k1.
Rep last row 12 times more—39 sts.
Dec row K1, [ssk] twice, k to last 5 sts, [k2tog] twice, k1—4 sts dec'd.
Rep last row 5 times more—15 sts. Pm at end of row for base of strap.
Change to dpn and work in garter st (k every row) on rem 15 sts until strap measures 3"/7.5cm from marker.
Dec row K1, ssk, k to last 3 sts, k2tog, k1—13 sts.
Cont in garter st until strap measures 5"/12.5cm from marker, rep dec row—11 sts.
Cont in garter st until strap measures 16"/40.5cm. Place sts on holder.

Back Handle
Rejoin yarn to WS, work 65 back sts same as for front.

Finishing
Graft or use 3-needle bind-off (see page 173) to join strap ends tog.
Weave in ends. Block to measurements. ■

EASY TO HANDLE
Make the handles as long or as short as you please by working more or fewer garter rows until you reach the desired length.

Cup Cozy Quartet

DESIGNED BY Audrey Drysdale

Choose your favorite stitch for a comfy cup cozy perfect for small/medium to-go cups. The button version accommodates a standard-size mug.

MEASUREMENTS
Width 8"/20.5cm
Length 4"/10cm

MATERIALS
- 3oz/80g and 197yd/180m skein of any acrylic/wool blend (4)
- 1 skein in White
- One pair size 7 (4.5mm) needles, *or size to obtain gauges*
- Stitch marker
- 2 buttons per cozy (optional)

GAUGES
- 17 sts and 30 rows to 4"/10cm over garter st using size 7 (4.5mm) needles.
- 19 sts and 25 rows to 4"/10cm over St st using size 7 (4.5mm) needles
TAKE TIME TO CHECK YOUR GAUGES.

NOTES
1) One skein will give you four cozies. Go ahead and give all four patterns a try.
2) Cozies are written for one size to fit average mug with handle or 12-16oz size take-out coffee cup.

GARTER COZY
Cast on 18 sts. Work in garter st (k every row) for 8"/20.5cm, end with a WS row. Bind off or proceed to add buttons.

Add Buttons (optional)
Next row (RS) Work pat over 4 sts, bind off 2 sts, work pat until last 6 sts, bind off 2 sts, work pat to end.
Next row Work pat, casting on 2 sts over bound-off sts.
Work 3 rows in pat. Bind off in pat.

Finishing
Weave in ends.
For unbuttoned version, sew cast-on and bound-off edges tog.
For buttoned version, sew buttons opposite buttonholes.

SEED STITCH COZY
Cast on 18 sts.
Row 1 (RS) *K1, p1; rep from * to end.
Row 2 *P1, k1; rep from * to end.
Rep rows 1 and 2 for seed st until piece measures 8½"/21.5cm from beg, end with a WS row. Bind off in pat OR add buttons same as for garter cozy.

Finishing
Weave in ends.
For unbuttoned version, sew cast-on and bound-off edges tog.
For buttoned version, sew buttons opposite buttonholes.

BOX STITCH COZY
Cast on 20 sts.
Row 1 (RS) *K2, p2, rep from * to last 2 sts, k2.
Rows 2 and 3 *P2, k2; rep from * to last 2 sts, p2.
Row 4 *K2, p2; rep from * to last 2 sts, k2.
Rep rows 1-4 for box st until piece measures 8½"/21.5cm from beg, end with a WS row. Bind off in pat OR add buttons same as for garter cozy.

Finishing
Weave in ends.
For unbuttoned version, sew cast-on and bound-off edges tog.
For buttoned version, sew buttons opposite buttonholes.

TEXTURED CHECK COZY
Cast on 19 sts.
Row 1 (RS) K3, *p1, k3; rep from * to end.
Row 2 K1, *p1, k3; rep from * to last 2 sts, p1, k1.
Rows 3-6 Rep rows 1 and 2 twice more.
Row 7 K1, *p1, k3; rep from * to last 2 sts, p1, k1.
Row 8 K3, *p1, k3; rep from * to end.
Rows 9-12 Rep rows 7 and 8 twice more.
Rep rows 1-12 for textured check pat until piece measures 8½"/21.5cm from beg. Bind off in pat OR add buttons same as for garter cozy.

Finishing
Weave in ends.
For unbuttoned version, sew cast-on and bound-off edges tog. For buttoned version, overlap extra 5 rows and sew buttons opposite buttonholes. ■

AS LONG AS IT TAKES
Because these cozies are knit sideways, you can easily knit more or fewer rows to fit any cup.

Dog Coat

DESIGNED BY Jil Eaton

This striped coat—with contrast ribbing piping the head, leg, and body openings—begins at the neck. Put it on your dog a few times as work progresses to check the fit.

SIZES
Small (Medium). Shown in size Medium.

MEASUREMENTS
Chest 14 (15)"/35.5 (38)cm
Length (neck to tail) 16 (18)"/40.5 (45.5)cm

MATERIALS
- 1¾oz/50g and 77yd/70m skein of any superwash wool (4)
- 1 skein each Aquamarine (A), Chartreuse (B), and Yellow (C)
- One pair size 8 (5mm) needles, *or size to obtain gauge*
- One set (4) size 8 (5mm) double-pointed needles (dpn)
- Stitch markers
- Stitch holders

GAUGE
18 sts and 24 rows to 4"/10cm over St st using size 8 (5mm) needles.
TAKE TIME TO CHECK YOUR GAUGE.

STRIPE PATTERN
In St st, *work 2 rows A, 2 rows B; rep from * for stripe pat.

K1, P1 RIB
Row 1 *K1, p1; rep from * to end.
Row 2 K the knit sts and p the purl sts.
Rep row 2 for k1, p1 rib.

DOG SWEATER
With straight needles and C, beg at neck, cast on 41 (45) sts.
Work in k1, p1 rib for 1½"/4cm, inc 22 sts evenly across last WS row—63 (67) sts.
Beg stripe pat and work until piece measures 4½"/11.5cm from beg, end with a WS row.

Divide for Leg Openings
Next row (RS) K8 (9), place rem sts on st holder.
Cont in stripe pat on only these 8 (9) sts for 3½"/9cm, end with a RS row. Place sts on a 2nd st holder.

Place next 38 (40) sts from first st holder on needle, leaving rem sts on holder. Rejoin yarn, bind off next 9 sts for first leg opening, k29 (31).
Cont in stripe pat on only these 29 (31) sts for 3½"/9cm, end with a RS row. Place sts on a 3rd st holder.

Place rem sts from first holder on needle. Rejoin yarn, and bind off next 9 sts for 2nd leg opening.
Cont in stripe pat on only rem 8 (9) sts for 3½"/9cm, end with a RS row.
Next row (WS) Cont in stripe pat, p8 (9), cast on 9 sts, work 29 (31) sts from 3rd holder, cast on 9 sts, work rem 8 (9) sts from 2nd holder.
Cont on 63 (67) sts until piece measures 11 (13½)"/28 (34.5)cm. Place markers at each end of this row.

Tail Shaping
Cont in stripe pat, bind off 5 sts at beg of next 2 rows, then 2 sts at beg of next 4 rows. Dec 1 st each edge every other row 9 times—27 (31) sts. Place sts on st holder.

Lower Border
With RS facing, straight needles, and C, beg at first marker and pick up and k 30 sts evenly along side edge, k27 (31) sts from holder, pick up and k 30 sts to 2nd marker—87 (91) sts.
Work in k1, p1 rib for 1"/2.5cm.
Bind off in rib.

Leg Opening Borders
With RS facing, dpn, and C, pick up and k 46 sts evenly around a leg opening. Join, and pm for beg of rnd.
Dec rnd Work in k1, p1 rib, dec 6 sts evenly around—40 sts.
Cont in k1, p1 rib for 1"/2.5cm.
Bind off in rib.
Rep for 2nd leg opening.

Finishing
Weave in ends. Sew center seam.

MAKE WAY
If your dog wears a harness, you can add a hole in the coat so the leash can hook onto it. Bind off stitches where the hook will fall, and then cast them back on the following row (effectively making a buttonhole).

Techniques & How-To
Cast-Ons

KNIT CAST-ON

This is a classic cast-on that many people like to use if a particular cast-on is not specified in the pattern instructions.

Make a slipknot on the left needle. *Insert the right needle knitwise into the stitch on the left needle. Wrap the yarn around the right needle as if to knit.

Draw the yarn through the first stitch to make a new stitch, but do not drop the stitch from the left needle.

Slip the new stitch to the left needle as shown. Repeat from the * until the required number of stitches is cast on.

CABLE CAST-ON

This cast-on creates a nice twist-like look along the bottom edge. It is sturdy yet elastic, making it useful for ribbed edges.

Cast on 2 stitches using the knit-on cast on described above. *Insert the right needle between the 2 stitches on the left needle.

Wrap the yarn around the right needle as if to knit and pull the yarn through to make a new stitch.

Place the new stitch on the left needle as shown. Repeat from the *, always inserting the right needle in between the last 2 stitches on the left needle.

Provisional Cast-On

A provisional cast-on is often used when you need to work from the cast-on edge a second time. Such instances include working in the opposite direction or creating a double-thick hem.

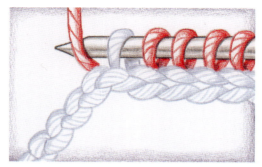

With scrap yarn and crochet hook, chain the number of stitches to cast on plus a few extra. Cut a tail and pull the tail through the last chain. With knitting needle and yarn, pick up and knit the stated number of stitches through the "bumps" on the back of the chain.

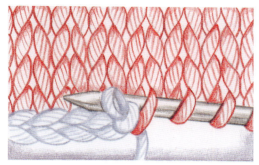

To remove the scrap yarn chain, when instructed, pull out the tail from the last crochet stitch. Gently and slowly pull on the tail to unravel the crochet stitches, carefully placing each released knit stitch on a needle.

Once all stitches are placed on the needle, Join new yarn and work the live stitches as instructed.

Increases

M1R AND M1R P-ST

M1R creates a right-leaning knit stitch and is detailed here. If you need to make M1R p-st, a right-leaning purl stitch, simply purl into the front loop in step 2.

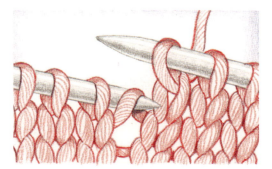

Insert the left needle from back to front under the horizontal strand between the last stitch worked and the next stitch on the left needle.

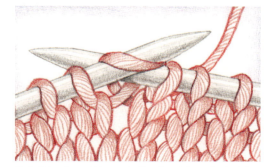

Knit this strand through the front loop to twist the stitch.

169

M1(L) AND M1(L) P-ST

M1 and M1L are the same increase that creates a left-leaning knit stitch. Some designers use M1L if both left- and right-leaning increases are used in the same pattern to help differentiate how each increase leans. If you need to make M1(L) p-st, a left-leaning purl stitch, simply purl into the back loop in step 2.

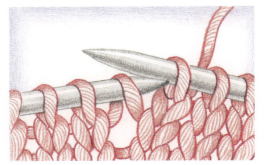

Insert the left needle from front to back under the horizontal strand between the last stitch worked and the first stitch on the left needle.

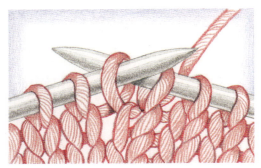

Knit this strand through the back loop to twist it.

KFB AND PFB

KFB stands for "Knit into the Front loop and Back loop." Doing so will increase one stitch. To work the PFB, which means to "Purl into the Front loop and Back loop," you will work in a similar fashion except inserting your needle purlwise and purling through both loops.

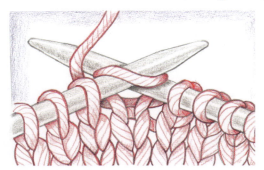

Insert the right needle knitwise into the front loop of the stitch. Wrap the yarn around the right needle and pull it through as if knitting, but leave the stitch on the left needle.

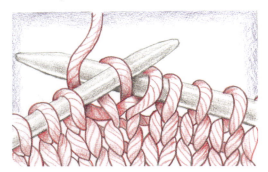

Insert the right needle knitwise into the back loop of the same stitch. Wrap the yarn around the needle and pull it through. Slip the stitch from the left needle.

Decreases

K2TOG AND P2TOG

K2tog and p2tog mean to knit or purl 2 stitches together. This is a very easy way to decrease 1 stitch. Similarly, you can decrease 2 stitches at a time by working a k3tog or p3tog decrease, where the only different is that you insert your needle into 3 stitches instead of 2.

To knit 2 stitches together, insert the right needle knitwise into the next 2 stitches on the left needle. Wrap the yarn around the right needle and pull it through.

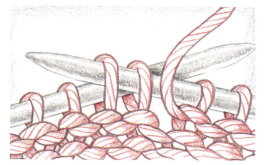

To purl 2 stitches together, insert the right needle purlwise into the next 2 stitches on the left needle. Wrap the yarn around the right needle and pull it through.

SKP

The SKP decreases 1 stitch. It is worked similarly to the S2KP, except that you only slip 1 stitch. SKP stands for "Slip 1 stitch, Knit 1 stitch, Pass slipped stitch over. the Knit 1 stitch". Knowing this can help you remember how to work it.

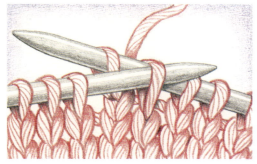

Slip 1 stitch knitwise, then knit the next stitch. Insert the left needle into the slipped stitch as shown.

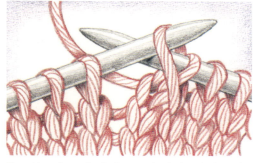

Pass the slipped stitch over the knit stitch and off the right needle.

SSK

The SSK decreases 1 stitch, slating to the right. SSK stands for "Slip 1, Slip 1, Knit 2 slipped stitches together." Knowing this can help you remember how to work it.

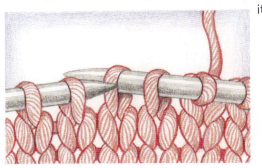

Slip 2 stitches knitwise, 1 at a time, from the left needle to the right needle.

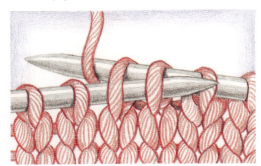

Insert the left needle into the fronts of these 2 slipped stitches as shown, and knit them together.

SSP

The SSP decreases 1 stitch, slating to the right. SSP stands for "slip 1, slip 1, purl 2 together." Knowing this can help you remember how to work it.

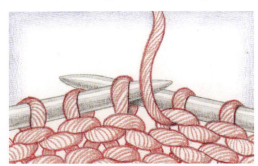

Slip 2 stitches knitwise, one at a time, from the left needle to the right needle. Return these 2 slipped stitches to the left needle as shown, keeping them twisted..

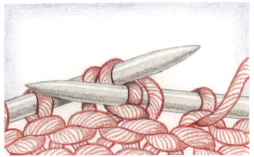

Purl these 2 stitches together through the back loops.

Bind-Offs

3-NEEDLE BIND-OFF

This method joins and binds off two separate sets of live stitches all at once. This can be worked over two separate pieces of knitting or two halves of a single piece. As its name suggests, a third needle is required for this bind-off.

First, make sure there is an equal number of stitches to be joined and bound off on each piece or half. Hold each set of stitches on a separate needle with the tip of each needle pointing to the right.

You will most often hold the right sides of each piece or half together, which will cause the seam to be hidden on the wrong side. However, if you wish for the seam to show on the right side, then you should hold the wrong sides of the pieces or halves together.

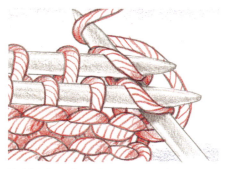

Hold right sides of pieces together on two needles. Insert third needle knitwise into first st of each needle, and wrap yarn knitwise.

Knit these two sts together, and slip them off the needles. *Knit the next two sts together in the same manner.

Slip first st on 3rd needle over 2nd st and off needle.

Rep from * in step 2 across row until all sts are bound off.

173

Short-Row Wrap & Turn (w&t)

Short-rows are partial rows that add more fabric in specific places of a knit piece, often for shaping, without increasing or decreasing stitches. The wrap-and-turn method, described here, has you work to a specific stitch, wrap that stitch, and then turn your fabric and work your way across the opposite side. These wraps help smooth the transitions between full and short-rows and prevent holes in the fabric. When you need to work over a wrapped stitch, work the stitch and its wrap together as one stitch.

WRAPPING A KNIT STITCH

With the yarn in back, slip the next stitch purlwise.

Move the yarn between the needles to the front of the work.

Slip the same stitch back to the left needle and turn the work. One knit stitch is wrapped.

If necessary to work the next stitch of the next row, bring the yarn between the needles to the front of the work. Otherwise, work the row as usual.

When you must knit a wrapped knit stitch, insert the right needle under the wrap and into the wrapped stitch, and knit them together.

WRAPPING A PURL STITCH

With the yarn in front, slip the next stitch purlwise.

Move the yarn between the needles to the back of the work.

Slip the same stitch back to the left needle and turn your work. One purl stitch is wrapped.
If necessary to work the next stitch in the next row, bring the yarn between the needles to the front of the work. Otherwise, work the next row as usual.

When you must purl a wrapped purl stitch, insert the right needle from behind into the back loop of the wrap and place it on the left needle, as shown. Purl the wrap together with the wrapped stitch on the left needle.

Kitchener Stitch

Kitchener stitch is a method of grafting two sets of live stitches together in a seamless fashion.

First, make sure your stitches are divided over two needles. If grafting stitches together on the same item, make sure the stitches are along opposite sides (ie. front and back). Thread a length of yarn that is at least 4 times the length of the edge that is to be grafted onto a tapestry needle. This can be the final tail of the project or a new length of yarn. Now you will feed the yarn through the live stitches following the path the yarn would have taken if it had been a knitted row as stated below.

KITCHENER STITCH OVER STOCKINETTE STITCH

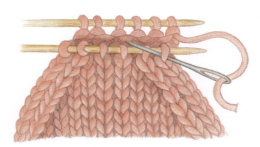

Insert tapestry needle purlwise through first stitch on front needle. Pull yarn through, leaving stitch on needle.

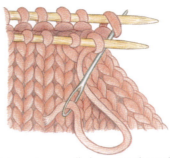

Insert tapestry needle knitwise through first stitch on back needle. Pull yarn through, leaving stitch on needle.

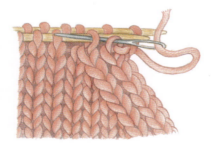

Insert tapestry needle knitwise through first stitch on front needle, pull yarn through, and slip stitch off needle. Then, insert tapestry needle purlwise through next stitch on front needle and pull yarn through, leaving this stitch on needle.

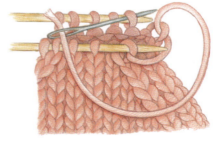

Insert tapestry needle purlwise through first stitch on back needle, pull yarn through, and slip stitch off needle. Then, insert tapestry needle knitwise through next stitch on back needle and pull yarn through, leaving this stitch on needle.

Repeat steps 3 and 4 until all stitches on both front and back needles have been grafted.

KITCHENER STITCH OVER GARTER STITCH

These illustrations show working over stitches that have been removed from their needles. If working stitches on needles, slip each stitch off the needle the second time it has been worked into.

Insert the yarn needle purlwise into the first stitch on the front piece, then purlwise into the first stitch on the back piece. Draw the yarn through.

Insert the yarn needle knitwise into the first stitch on the front piece again. Draw the yarn through.

Insert the yarn needle purlwise into the next stitch on the front piece. Draw the yarn through.

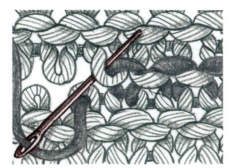

Insert the yarn needle knitwise into the first stitch on the back piece again. Draw the yarn through.

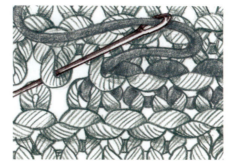

Insert the yarn needle purlwise into the next stitch on the back piece. Draw the yarn through.

Repeat steps 2 through 5.

Joining in the Round

Working in the round allows you to knit tubular pieces such as hats and sleeves. To begin, cast on the required number of stitches and then "join." To join means to bring the last cast-on stitch to the first cast-on stitch to create a closed loop of stitches from which you will knit rounds.

Whether you are working on double-pointed needles or a circular needle, when you join you must make sure the stitches are not twisted. If your stitches are twisted around your needle(s) when you join, your fabric will be twisted and unusable. Align the ridge opposite the loops of the stitches to the center of the circular needle or double-pointed needles.

Correct

Correct

Incorrect

Next, work the first cast-on stitch, pulling the yarn tightly so there is no gap between the last cast-on stitch and the first worked stitch of the first round (see Join 1 an Join 2).

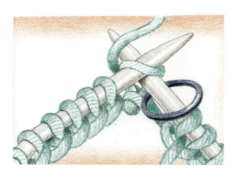
Joining on a Circular Needle

Joining on Double-Pointed Needles

Another way to make a neat join is to cast on one extra stitch. Bring the first and last cast-on stitches together, and then slip the extra stitch to the first needle. Work the extra stitch and the first cast-on stitch together as the first stitch in the first round. This removes the extra stitch you cast on so you have the correct number of stitches.

Whether you are working on a circular needle or any number of double-pointed needles, you can use either method of joining listed here.

Blocking

Blocking evens out your stitches and makes sure your project will be the correct size and shape. This is especially important for projects that require good fit, such as a sweater.

There are a few of methods of blocking, and even though they produce the same result you should use whichever method is best for the yarn. Because different fibers react differently to heat and the various methods of blocking, check the yarn label for blocking guidance. It is advisable to block your gauge swatch to see how the fabric will react.

WET BLOCK

Immerse the piece in cool or warm water and gently handwash the fabric to even out your stitches and settle them in place. Let the piece soak for a few minutes, then press out the water. **Never wring out a knitted fabric.** Fold the knit and squeeze out the excess water. To get out even more water, wrap it in a towel and then press again. Next, lay the piece on an ironing board or blocking mats, and then pin it to the appropriate size and shape. Leave it to dry.

WET BLOCK BY SPRAYING

Lay the piece on an ironing board or blocking mats, and pin it to the appropriate size and shape. With a spray bottle of cool or warm water, spritz the piece until it is damp. Let the piece dry.

STEAM BLOCK

Lay the piece on an ironing board or blocking mats, pin it to the appropriate size and shape. With a steamer or steam iron, blast steam onto the piece. If using a steam iron, do not let it touch the piece, simply hold it near. Once the piece is damp, smooth out any remaining bumps by hand and leave it to dry.

Once your piece is dry, unpin it. It should retain the shape and size at which it was blocked.

BLOCKING FIBER GUIDE

These are some common yarn fibers and how they are often blocked. However, you should always check the yarn label for blocking guidance for your specific yarn.

- **Cotton:** Wet block or warm/hot steam block.
- **Linen:** Wet block or warm/hot steam block.
- **Mohair:** Wet block by spraying.
- **Novelties (highly textured):** Do not block.
- **Synthetics:** Carefully follow instructions on ball band—usually wet block by spraying.
- **Wool and all animal fibers (alpaca, camel hair, cashmere):** Wet block or warm steam block.
- **Wool blends:** Wet block by spraying.

Seaming

There are many different ways to seam (or sew) together knit pieces. Some patterns list a specific method to use while others do not. If no particular method is listed, choose your preferred method. Some methods are to be worked over specific stitch patterns and edge types for specific results. Consider your pieces, the edges being joined, the direction in which the edges will be joined, and proceed accordingly.

HOW TO BEGIN SEAMING

If you have left a long tail from your cast-on row, you can use this strand to begin sewing. To make a neat join at the lower edge with no gap, use the technique shown here.

Thread the strand into a yarn needle. With the right sides of both pieces facing you, insert the yarn needle from back to front, into the corner stitch of the piece without the tail. Making a figure eight with the yarn, insert the needle from back to front into the stitch from the cast-on tail. Tighten to close the gap.

INVISIBLE HORIZONTAL SEAM

This seam is used to join two bound-off edges, such as shoulder seams, and is worked stitch by stitch. You must have the same number of stitches on each piece. Pull the yarn tightly enough to hide the bound-off edges. The finished seam resembles a row of knit stitches.

With the bound-off edges together, lined up stitch for stitch, insert the yarn needle under a stitch inside the bound-off edge of one side and then under the corresponding stitch on the other side.

The finished horizontal seam on stockinette stitch.

INVISIBLE VERTICAL TO HORIZONTAL SEAM

This seam is used to join bound-off stitches to rows, as in sewing the top of a sleeve to an armhole edge. Because there are usually more rows per inch (2.5 cm) than stitches, occasionally pick up two horizontal bars on the piece with rows for every stitch on the bound-off piece.

Insert the yarn needle under a stitch inside the bound-off edge of the vertical piece. Insert the needle under one or two horizontal bars between the first and 2nd stitches of the horizontal piece.

The finished vertical to horizontal seam on stockinette stitch.

MATTRESS STITCH OVER GARTER

This invisible seam is worked on garter stitch. It is similar to the seam worked on reverse stockinette stitch in that you alternate working into the top and bottom loops of the stitches.

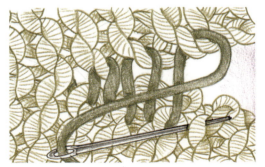

Insert the yarn needle into the top loop on one side, then in the bottom loop of the corresponding stitch on the other side. Continue to alternate in this way.

The finished vertical seam on garter stitch.

181

MATTRESS STITCH OVER REVERSE STOCKINETTE STITCH

As with stockinette stitch, this invisible seam is worked from the right side, row by row, but instead of working into the horizontal strand between stitches, you work into the stitch itself. Alternate working into the top loop on one side with the bottom loop on the other side.

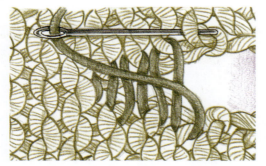

Working into the stitches inside the edge, insert the yarn needle into the top loop on one side, then in the bottom loop of the corresponding stitch on the other side. Continue to alternate in this way.

The finished vertical seam on reverse stockinette stitch.

MATTRESS STITCH OVER STOCKINETTE STITCH

This invisible vertical seam is worked from the right side and is used to join two edges row by row. It hides the uneven selvage stitches at the edge of a row and creates an invisible seam, making it appear that the knitting is continuous.

Working into the stitches inside the edge, insert the yarn needle into the top loop on one side, then in the bottom loop of the corresponding stitch on the other side. Continue to alternate in this way.

The finished vertical seam on stockinette stitch.

OVERCAST STITCH

This seam is usually worked from the wrong side, but it can also be worked from the right side with a thick yarn in a contrasting color to create an exposed decorative, cordlike seam.

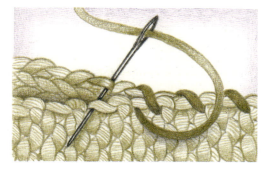

With the right sides of the pieces facing each other and the bumps lined up, insert the needle from back to front through the strands at the edges of the pieces between the knots. Repeat this step.

The finished overcast seam on stockinette stitch.

Embroidery Stitches

Embroidery is a great way to add extra detail to your knits. Thread your desired color of yarn onto a tapestry needle and work as detailed below. Keep all ends on the wrong side of the work, weaving them in once the embroidery is complete.

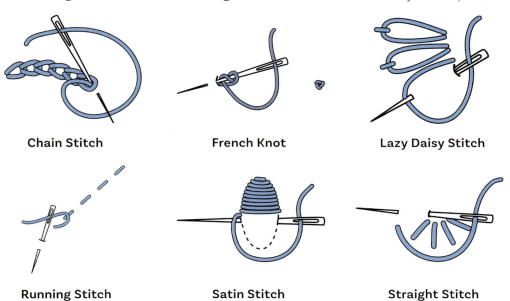

Chain Stitch   **French Knot**   **Lazy Daisy Stitch**

Running Stitch   **Satin Stitch**   **Straight Stitch**

Index

#
3-Needle Bind Off 173

A
Abbreviations 10
Accessories
    Cabled Baby Booties 46
    Classic Mittens 36
    Color-Tipped Slippers 50
    Diamonds Headband 52
    Fingerless Mitts 42
    Hedgehog Slippers 48
    Planted Headband 54
    Shell Rib Wristers 40
    Sweet Stripes Baby Booties 44
Accordion Rib Hat & Mitts 32
All Angles Wrap 58

B
Basketweave Hat 20
Bind off
    3 Needle Bind Off 173
Blanket
    Bunny Buddy Blanket 134
    Candy Cabin Afghan & Pillow 150
    Chevron Pop Blanket 140
    Garden Patch Lapghan 146
    Garter Gingham Blanket 148
    Garter Stripes Blanket 129
    Gridded Blanket 138
    Purl Stitch Snowflake Blanket 142
    Shifting Chevron Blanket 154
    Stained Glass Blanket 132
    Stronger Together Blanket 136
    Turtle Lace Blanket 144
Blaze Pullover 88
Blocking
Blocking Fiber Guide 179
    Steam Block 179
    Wet Block 179
Bow Scarf 78
Brioche Watch Cap 26
Bunny Buddy Blanket 134
Buttoned Poncho Cardigan 114

C
Cabled Baby Booties 46
Cable Cast On 168
Candy Cabin Afghan & Pillow 150
Cardigan
    Buttoned Poncho Cardigan 114
    Garter-Stitch Baby Cardigan 126
    Perforated Cardigan 118
    Shawl-Collar Cardigan 106
    Summer Cardigan 122
    Winter Haze Cardigan 110
Cast-Ons
    Cable Cast On 168
    Knit Cast On 168
    Provisional Cast On 169
Chain Stitch 183
Chevron Pop Blanket 140
Chevron Pullover 91
Classic Mittens 36
Color-Tipped Slippers 50
Cowl
    Textured Cowl 80
Cup Cozy Quartet 164

D
Decreases
    K2tog 171
    P2tog 171
    SKP 171
    Ssk 172
    Ssp 172
Diagonal Ridge Shawl 56
Diamonds Headband 52
Dipper Shawl 64
Dog Coat 166
Double Swiss Shawl 69

E
Embroidery Stitches
    Chain Stitch 183
    French Knot 183
    Lazy Daisy Stitch 183
    Running Stitch 183
    Satin Stitch 183
    Straight Stitch 183

F
Fingerless Mitts 42
French Knot 183

G
Garden Patch Lapghan 146
Garter Gingham Blanket 148
Garter-Stitch Baby Cardigan 126
Garter Stitch Basket 156
Garter Stripes Blanket 129
Gridded Blanket 138

H
Hat
    Accordion Rib Hat & Mitts 32
    Basketweave Hat 20
    Brioche Watch Cap 26
    Lace Tam 24
    Oval Twist Hat & Scarf 30
    Rib Duo Watch Cap 14
    Staggered Rib Hat 16
    Super Bulky Hat 12
    Toasty Tot Hat 22
    Torsades Beret 28
    Twisted Rib Hat 18
Hedgehog Slippers 48
Honey Pullover 97
How to Use This Book 9
Hound's Tooth Scarf 74

I
Increases
    Kfb 170
    M1R 169
    M1R P-St 169
    M1(L) 170
    M1(L) p-st 170
    Pfb 170
Introduction 8

J
Joining in the Round 178

K
K2tog 171
Kfb 170
Kitchener Stitch 176
    Over Garter Stitch 177
    Over Stockinette 176
Knit Cast On 168

L
Lace Tam 24
Lazy Daisy Stitch 183

M
M1R 169
M1R p-st 69
M1(L) 170
M1(L) p-st 170
Malibu Ripple Shawl 62

O
On the Market 162
Opposites Dolman Pullover 82
Oval Twist Hat & Scarf 30
Overcast Stitch 183

P
P2tog 171
Pebble Yoke Pullover 85
Peek-a-Boo Lace Shawl 66
Perforated Cardigan 118
Pfb 170
Planted Headband 54
Pocket Scarf 76
Potted Plant Cozies 160
Provisional Cast On 169
Pullover
    Blaze Pullover 88
    Chevron Pullover 91
    Honey Pullover 97
    Opposites Dolman Pullover 82
    Pebble Yoke Pullover 85
    Pumpkin Spice Pullover 103
    Snowfall Sweater 94
    Toasty Tot Sweater 100
Pumpkin Spice Pullover 103
Purl Stitch Snowflake Blanket 142

R
Rib Duo Watch Cap 14
Running Stitch 183

S
Satin Stitch 183
Scarf
    Bow Scarf 78
    Hound's Tooth Scarf 74
    Pocket Scarf 76
Seaming
    How to Begin Seaming 180
    Invisible Horizontal Seam 180
    Invisible Vertical to Horizontal Seam 181
    Mattress Stitch over Garter 181
    Mattress Stitch over Reverse Stockinette Stitch 182
    Mattress Stitch over Stockinette Stitch 182
    Overcast Stitch 183
Shawl
    Diagonal Ridge Shawl 56
    Dipper Shawl 64
    Double Swiss Shawl 69
    Malibu Ripple Shawl 62
    Peek-a-Boo Lace Shawl 66
    Shifting Tides Scarf 72
    Theatre Shawl 60
Shawl-Collar Cardigan 106
Shell Rib Wristers 40
Shifting Chevron Blanket 154
Shifting Tides Scarf 72
Short Row Wrap and Turn 174
SKP 171
Snowfall Sweater 94
Ssk 172
Ssp 172
Staggered Rib Hat 16
Stained Glass Blanket 132
Straight Stitch 183
Stronger Together Blanket 136
Super Bulky Hat 12
Summer Cardigan 122
Sweet Stripes Baby Booties 44

T
Textured Cowl 80
Textured Washcloths 158
Theatre Shawl 60
Toasty Tot Hat 22
Toasty Tot Sweater 100
Torsades Beret 28
Turtle Lace Blanket 144
Twisted Rib Hat 18

W
Wrap
    All Angles Wrap 58
Winter Haze Cardigan 110